mardi gras indians

LOUISIANA TRUE books tell the stories of the state's iconic places, traditions, foods, and objects. Each book centers on one element of Louisiana's culture, unpacking the myths, misconceptions, and historical realities behind everything that makes our state unique, from aboveground cemeteries to zydeco.

PREVIOUS BOOKS IN THE SERIES

Mardi Gras Beads

Brown Pelican

mardi gras indians

NIKESHA ELISE WILLIAMS

Louisiana State University Press

Baton Rouge

Published by Louisiana State University Press
lsupress.org

LSU Press Paperback Original

Manufactured in the United States of America
First printing

Designer: Barbara Neely Bourgoyne
Typeface: Source Sans Variable
Printer and binder: Integrated Books International (IBI)

Cover illustration: Mardi Gras Indian at Jazz Fest, 2011 (modified). Courtesy Albert Herring, Tulane Public Relations / Wikimedia Commons.

Library of Congress Cataloging-in-Publication Data
Names: Williams, Nikesha Elise, author.
Title: Mardi Gras Indians / Nikesha Elise Williams.
Other titles: Louisiana true.
Description: Baton Rouge : Louisiana State University Press, [2023] | Series: Louisiana true | Includes bibliographical references.
Identifiers: LCCN 2022014734 (print) | LCCN 2022014735 (ebook) | ISBN 978-0-8071-7870-6 (paperback) | ISBN 978-0-8071-7913-0 (pdf) | ISBN 978-0-8071-7912-3 (epub)
Subjects: LCSH: Mardi Gras Indians—Social life and customs. | Mardi Gras Indians—History. | African Americans—Louisiana—New Orleans—History.
Classification: LCC F380.B53 W55 2022 (print) | LCC F380.B53 (ebook) | DDC 976.3/3500496073—dc23/eng/20220420
LC record available at https://lccn.loc.gov/2022014734
LC ebook record available at https://lccn.loc.gov/2022014735

IN MEMORY OF BIG CHIEF KEELIAN BOYD

Also known as Big Chief Dump, who died on March 28, 2021, from heart failure. He was thirty-seven years old. Boyd was known as "The Hat Man" and "The Hook Up" man in the Indian tradition for the elaborate crowns he constructed, and for being able to put together suits for Indians—still building, beading, and sewing until the very last moment. Boyd masked for twenty-three years. *Courtesy Matthew Hinton.*

contents

preface

Food is my love language. The first inklings of this text began with food, specifically with my love for New Orleans–style red beans and rice. A personal essay I wrote about that dish led to me being contacted by LSU Press regarding their project of publishing books about different aspects of Louisiana culture. An unsolicited query in my inbox asked, “Are you interested?”

“Of course,” I responded.

However, I didn’t want to write about food as I had done in other essays. I knew immediately that I wanted to write about the Indians, but I agreed to look at the list of subjects the Press wanted to cover before making a final decision. As a New Orleanian once removed, similar to how author and journalist Isabel Wilkerson referred to herself in her book *The Warmth of Other Suns,* I shared the list with my mother, a New Orleans native. She said, “The only thing on this list I know I can help you with is the Indians.”

Opposite: Wild Tchoupitoulas Indian gang masked for Carnival in 2018. Courtesy Erroll Lebeau.

Her statement in March 2020 solidified what I would be writing about. I began my preliminary research with Google. The search engine immediately spat back at me dozens of newspaper stories on Mardi Gras and COVID; the global pandemic was still in its nascent stages in the United States. When I started this search to write the book proposal, Ronald W. Lewis, the founder of the renowned Museum of Dance and Feathers, was still alive. By the time I finished the proposal and submitted it in early April, he had died. The news of his death led me deeper into my family, as Lewis was the uncle of my cousin, Brent Taylor.

As the news of my project spread through my family like hot gossip after Sunday service, my father, also a New Orleans native, as well as aunts and cousins all suggested names I should look up and people I should speak with. My father's suggestion: "You gotta watch the documentary *Tootie's Last Suit.* Tootie was the prettiest Indian ever."

My aunt Mary Ryan said: "My next-door neighbor Charmon, her nephew is a Big Chief; his name is Romeo. You gotta get in contact with him. He's on Facebook."

Other names I wanted to follow up on were those I kept seeing in the results of my Google search: Bo Dollis and Donald Harrison. Though both men had already passed, their children were still carrying on the tradition.

From my home in Jacksonville, Florida, I planned a trip to New Orleans in the middle of a global pandemic. I set up visits to archives and made preliminary contact with Romeo, the Mardi Gras Indian Council, as well as the Backstreet Cultural Museum. I planned to wing the rest of it once I got on the ground in the city. My mother flew from Chicago to Florida. Then we drove the eight hours on I-10 from Jacksonville to New Orleans.

Once in the city, Stafford Agee came to my aunt Mary's house in the Seventh Ward and interviewed with me in the basement. I contacted Bo Dollis Jr. via Instagram, and he agreed to let me interview him at his townhouse in the East. My cousin Tanya Devey put me in contact with Keelian Boyd, whom she'd known for years. When I arrived at the home of his cousin Charles Duvernay, I interviewed them first before calling in their spouses.

Another cousin, L'Maun Morris, introduced me to Ronnel Butler. It was while I was out with L'Maun that I caught up with my cousin Brent at Ronald W. Lewis's home. Though his wife was still grieving and didn't want to interview with me, she and Brent did allow me to walk through the museum and take notes and pictures as I pleased. During this walk-through I met Gilbert "Cosmo" Dave. He, too, was still grieving the loss of his best friend, but he agreed to open his heart and speak to me about the culture and the tradition. While still at the House of Dance and Feathers, Romeo messaged me that he was finally ready to talk. My interview with Cherice Harrison-Nelson took place after my trip to New Orleans as she was busy during my time there and did not want to meet in person because of COVID precautions. At the time of my visit, she participated in the memorial service for the late Joe Jenkins.

However, this cadre of interviews didn't provide me with enough material to write a book on a culture and tradition whose history spans centuries. During my visit to the Amistad Research Center, I was able to dig through the donated items from the Harrison family, many of which hadn't even been cataloged yet. It was there that I watched their family-produced documentary from the 1990s and received a link to watch the Maurice Martinez documentary from 1976. During my time digging through the archives at the Historic New Orleans Collection in the French Quarter, I returned to Google to find more primary sources. I ordered every book I could find. Jeroen Dewulf's *From the Kingdom of Kongo to Congo Square;* the biographies of Donald Harrison Sr. and Robert Nathaniel Lee by Al Kennedy; *Jockomo: The Native Roots of Mardi Gras Indians,* by Shane Lief and John McCusker; *Congo Square in New Orleans,* by Jerah Johnson, which I initially started reading in the archives; *Freedom's Dance,* with photographs by Eric Waters and narrative text by Karen Celestan; and *Mardi Gras Indians,* by Michael P. Smith—a book so rare the first time I searched for it it was priced at $120. The secondhand copy I eventually purchased, with someone else's name scrawled in marker on the inside, still cost me $65. I also picked up Ronald W. Lewis's book published in conjunction with the Neighborhood Story Project during my jaunt with my cousin L'Maun, and I ordered Victor Harris's book, also published with the Neighborhood Story Project months later.

With these sources and interviews I began reading and making notes. The history of the Indians I found mostly in the texts from Dewulf and Lief and McCusker. The latter led me to the historic newspaper articles that detailed the exploits of the Indians during Mardi Gras. Johnson's book helped to put into context the importance of Congo Square and how convergence upon the square by African and Indigenous people led to the intermixing and syncretizing of culture to birth the Black masking Indians. Meanwhile, the biographies of Donald Harrison Sr. and Robert Nathaniel Lee as well as the documentary *Tootie's Last Suit* gave first-person accounts from Indians who masked in the early days of the formal culture.

With these interviews, oral histories, documentaries, and other primary sources, I knew—as I stated in my proposal—that I had to dig into the history. But it became clear early in my research that the history would always be a mixed and muddled grouping of assumptions and assertions loosely held together by disparate corroborating documents. The history was no longer the crux of my questioning. My focus was this: How did this tradition survive? How is it still surviving? My thesis question was no longer when or why but how. For me, the evolution became much more important than the origin.

In this book, I have attempted to thread the needle between history and evolution as closely as possible using the resources available, most notably firsthand accounts. The culture of Black masking Indians is an oral tradition. I hope you will find that in this book the voices of Indians past and present have been heard.

mardi gras indians

Introduction

There is no single, definitive origin story that pinpoints the beginnings of what has been extrapolated over centuries into today's Black masking, or Mardi Gras, Indian culture. Instead, there is a multiplicity of stories that have more or less fidelity to a truth none of us were alive to know. The accuracy of these stories about what led African American men and women to mask themselves in feathers, beads, and bells a few times a year in the name of history, lineage, and legacy depends upon how wide or narrow the scope and perspective of the historian, researcher, biographer, or journalist telling the tale. It also depends upon which Indian from which tribe you're speaking with and what version of the story they were told that starts many generations before the oft-quoted 1886.

What is undeniable, however, is that New Orleans Black masking Indian culture is as African as it is Indigenous, as French as it is Spanish, and as American as are many other African American art forms that combine the sacred and secular, the spiritual and profane, the rebellious and resilient, and the tragedy, struggle, and protest of a people with its triumph, rejoicing, and jubilee. In short, New Orleans Mardi Gras Indian culture is an exemplary illustration of the American motto E pluribus unum. Out of many, one.

As Rachel Carrico and Esailama Artry Diouf noted in their chapter "Flying High" from Eric Waters and Karen Celestan's book *Freedom's Dance: Social Aid and Pleasure Clubs in New Orleans:* "The blending of African, European, and Native American styles and techniques of both music and dance has led to the evolution of new styles that have become indigenous to New Orleans; some of the styles have become a signature of the expressive culture of the United States. Cultural expressions performed at Congo Square and on the streets of New Orleans gradually developed into Mardi Gras Indian traditions, New Orleans Jazz, and rhythm and blues, and the Second Line."

This intertwining of Indigenous, African, European, Catholic, and African Traditional Religions that became African American culture as we know it today is a kismetic, predestined fatalism, keeping America from being the pure frontier of the WASP and thus producing the most celebrated American cultural feats: distinctive food, music, dancing, and language. These are unique cultural products that can all be seen in one of the country's greatest cities, New Orleans, and its secretive subset of Carnival culture, the Black masking Indians.

New Orleans Mardi Gras Indian culture was born out of necessity. It was birthed through the grit and determination of our ancestors on this continent, who realized that they were being colonized even while some of their own were complicit in that colonization through Christianity, in general, and Catholicism specifically.

Also, it is important to distinguish and delineate Mardi Gras Indian culture that is specific, endemic, and inherent to New Orleans. Although the culture is unique to the United States of America, in South America, the Caribbean, and the whole of the African diaspora, it is but one iteration of a syncretic spiritual and artistic form that has been sanitized and commodified for the tourism-driven economy of Carnival.

In this respect, New Orleans is not so much a southern state in the United States as it is "the northern periphery of a cultural field that had its center in South America." Having this wider worldview gives richer context to the seeming anomaly of New Orleans culture in comparison to the modest WASPy ways of the rest of the country, perhaps save for the Gullah Geechee in the South Carolina lowcountry. From jazz funerals, neighborhood second-line parades, and an active roster of social aid and pleasure clubs to our subject, Black masking Indians, these specific attributes of Black culture in New Orleans "are not a uniquely Louisianian product. Rather, they represent a specific variant of a much broader phenomenon that has been observed in many other parts of the Americas."

Another phenomenon that has been observed across the diaspora, in the American South, and New Orleans specifically, is the place, space, and function of rage. American literary icon James Baldwin said in 1961 that "to be a Negro in this country and to be relatively conscious is to be in a state of rage almost, almost all of the time—and in one's work." This is embodied in the culture, lifestyle, and life's work of every Mardi Gras Indian. This rage is present in every completed suit, every beaded patch, every 3D assemblage, and every golden crown placed atop the head with plumes, feathers, and marabou that sway regally with the subtle movements of each tribe member from the Wild Man and Spy Boy to the Big Chief.

This rage was present in the resistance of the Indigenous tribes who called the booming port city near the mouth of the Mississippi home. This rage was present in the rebellion of the enslaved Africans turned Black Americans who preserved their continental culture and customs despite the oppressive rigidity of Code Noir and the papal mandates of Catholicism. This rage was and is present in the opposition of today's Black masking Indians, who have dressed and paraded in the face of forced segregation, police harassment, relegated peonage despite integration, city politics over permits, hurricanes, and a pandemic.

Inside a suit of beads and feathers these men and women are Black and free, pretty and proud, and, most importantly, returned unto themselves; they are bridging the gap of erasure that was lost at every door of no return and on the many routes of the trail of tears. Inside their suits these Indians are whole and complete, restored, transformed, and even transcendent. They are their ancestors' wildest dreams personified. From the frenzied Sunday-afternoon gatherings in Congo Square of those both free and in bondage, to the heavily ritualized peace pipe ceremonies that spread among Indigenous groups up and down the Mississippi River, to the degradation put upon them by the parading Mistick Krewe of Comus, these men and women who dared to adorn themselves with baubles of beauty stand as a living testament to the resilience of the native spirit, be it Native American or African.

This spirit has been carried through the strands of DNA from generation to generation, imprinting the ancestors' wills and wishes into the souls of their progeny. It is the reason an encounter with the Mardi Gras Indians is described as "the deepest sense of connection between the ancient past and the living present."

In my research I have found that other ethnographic, anthropological, and historical researchers seem to have an intrinsic desire, if not dogged need, to prove without a doubt that they have found the evidence of the definitive origin of this parading culture in New Orleans that is mostly Black and unlike any other anywhere else in the United States. But there is no one definitive origin story. Rather, many different originations have contributed to the cultural gumbo we now know, see, and experience as the Mardi Gras Indians. Therefore, the question this text seeks to answer is not how, or when, or from whom the Mardi Gras Indians came to be, but how they managed to survive and, in their own words, what they see for themselves next.

This work seeks to not only venerate the various disparate strands of the ancient past that have led to the Mardi Gras Indians but also to shed light on their codified practices that have been in effect since the nineteenth century. Furthermore, this text will illustrate how the evolution of music, dance, social norms, and racial constructs have positioned the Mardi Gras Indians for an enduring future those currently masking cannot imagine, just like those who masked before them could not possibly fathom where the culture is now.

Through the perils of the transatlantic slave trade, the Indian Removal Act, Jim Crow, the persistent stigma of violence, the civil rights movement, Hurricanes Betsy and Katrina, and the scourge of COVID-19, vestiges of an ancient tradition at once spiritual, political, and communal have remained. This is the story of the evolution of those vestiges, staunchly held by the descendants of those who survived the aforementioned trials to remain the purveyors of history and culture by serving as griots in their communities, role models to children, and bastions of public service.

1

In the Beginning Was the World

The artists and art form we now know as Black masking Indians began in the days of old, in the times of ancient kingdoms the surface of whose history archaeologists and anthropologists have only begun to brush. In those days of antiquity in Africa and North America, in the Old World kingdoms of the Akan, Ashanti, Wolof, and Kongo, and the delegations of the Iroquois, Natchez, Chitimatcha, Cherokee, and Choctaw, the scenes of intricately beaded designs, feathered headdresses, ritual dancing, proud preparations for war, peaceful transitions of power and respect, and veneration given to ancestors and deities alike were first witnessed by the eyes of Europeans.

It was this observation, and these encounters between Africans and Europeans, and Native Americans and Europeans, that brought three distinct and seemingly dissimilar cultures together for a mash-up that has remained mysterious and is regressively reduced to a costume contest a few times a year. In actuality, what we witness today in the Mardi Gras Indians is a cultural system carefully curated over centuries that includes "a complex web of activities including sewing, dancing, drumming, engaging in public processions and private rituals—as well as special structural elements such as phrases, songs, a distinct social hierarchy and spirituality." This all began on its own in these old worlds; then there was an introduction, an infiltration, and, finally, a betrayal.

This history has not been widely documented. One of the first authors to take up the Mardi Gras Indians as a subject and explore the rich history of their tradition is New Orleans photographer Michael P. Smith in his 1994 book *Mardi Gras Indians.* In it, Smith explores the African and Creole roots of Black masking Indian men and women. His research has been expounded upon by University of California, Berkeley, associate professor Jeroen Dewulf. In his book *From the Kingdom of Kongo to Congo Square: Kongo Dances and the Origins of the Mardi Gras Indians,* Dewulf works to establish a direct connection between today's Mardi Gras Indians and the Kongolese people of Central Africa. Similarly, New Orleans natives Shane Lief and John McCusker, in their book *Jockomo: The Native Roots of Mardi Gras Indians,* spend time showing the definitive influences and origins of the Mardi Gras Indians as a cultural outgrowth of the Indigenous tribes who inhabited the lower Mississippi River valley in the eighteenth century.

There is a more than twenty-year gap between the publication of Smith's book and the publication of the works by Dewulf and Lief and McCusker. In that interim the storied history of the Mardi Gras Indians continued to be passed down in the way that it always had been—through oral tradition. Some of this oral history was captured by University of New Orleans professor Al Kennedy in his biographies of Mardi Gras Indian Big Chiefs Donald Harrison and Robert "Robbe" Nathaniel Lee. Documentarians also captured this history (as early as the 1970s) in sound and motion. These well-researched historical texts as well as these oral histories all point to the African roots of the Mardi Gras Indians as well as their Indigenous roots, reflected in the heavy influence of Native American garb.

These roots also include European elements, most notably Parisian Carnival culture, as well as Catholic procession culture. Today's Black masking Indian culture is therefore the result of the intermixing of these various root cultures that emerged once European colonizers encountered both individual groups and brought them together. For our subject specifically, this fusion of culture that developed into who and what we now know as Mardi Gras Indians happened gradually over time before exploding to brightly colored life in the mid- to late nineteenth century.

WHO ARE THE BLACK MASKING/MARDI GRAS INDIANS?

So far we've talked a lot about Mardi Gras/Black masking Indians and their culture in the abstract, but what and who exactly are they today? First, I use the terms "Mardi Gras Indians" and "Black masking Indians" interchangeably throughout this text to refer to our subject, the Black masking Indians of New Orleans. Although those outside of the culture refer to these groups as Mardi Gras Indians because Mardi Gras is when they appear most often and consistently, those inside the culture may refer to themselves differently.

"Me myself I don't consider myself a Mardi Gras Indian; I'm a

Black masking Indian," said Ronnel Butler, who holds the Gang Flag position with the 9th Ward Black Hatchet tribe. "A Black masking Indian, he can come out anytime he want to, anytime he feel, he can put his suit on when he feel like it because that's his culture, that's a part of his religion. That's what I feel."

Some also may prefer the term "Black masking Indian" because for years Black people were not allowed to wholly participate in the white Carnival and Mardi Gras celebrations New Orleans is famous for except in the capacity of flambeaux-bearers. Furthermore, not only were Black people not allowed to participate in the masking at Carnival, but many avoided going to the celebrations altogether because of the police brutality they would experience in the still deeply racist and segregated city. As Fred Johnson, former Spy Boy for the Yellow Pocahontas, said in the documentary *Tootie's Last Suit:* "What I remember about parades was a lot of problems. Racist police, brutality, just problems. You could get called a nigger, and if you get into a fight with them and the police come, the police gon' side with them, and you gon' get a double ass whipping. So you can have that, man! To go catch a pair of beads? No. Mmhmm."

Chief Victor "Fi Yi Yi" Harris of the Spirit of the Fi Yi Yi Mandingo Warriors echoed Johnson's sentiment: "I never experienced the white Carnival. Maybe when I was a child I used to go to the parade, before I started masking as a Mardi Gras Indian. Never went to the parade. Back in the day, prejudice was existing. It was hard for us to even go to the parade because we would get pushed around for no reason whatsoever. So, experiencing the white Carnival was hard for us because we wasn't accepted."

In these vignettes it's clear how and why the traditions of New Orleans Carnival season in the city's Black community developed separate and apart from the more Parisian-style Carnival happening uptown and in the French Quarter. In these dueling yet segregated Mardi Gras traditions, the Black masking Indians became a cornerstone of Black Carnival celebrations, even though today they are beloved by all, Black and white.

So who are the Black masking/Mardi Gras Indians of New Orleans?

The simplest answer is that they are groups of Black men and women who dress up in the style of the Plains Indians for Mardi Gras, St. Joseph's Night, Super Sunday, and other cultural celebrations throughout the calendar year. The groups known as tribes or gangs—and not in the criminal sense—are usually family members; family and friends; or family, friends, and neighbors. Each member of a tribe or gang holds a specific position. The Big Chief is the leader. The Spy Boy is the lookout. The Flag Boy carries the tribe's flag to announce their arrival on the street. The Wild Man is the mischief maker who can play anywhere throughout the formation of the tribe as they parade through the street. Tribe members spend their days sewing their elaborately decorated suits for their Carnival-centered appearances, and they have practices throughout the week where they go over secretive hand signals that allow them to communicate without speaking and dance and sing songs—new ones they've composed as well as traditional songs that have been passed down from generation to generation, most of them in English, though African, French and Indigenous words remain in the soundtrack of the culture.

Yet this, too, is an oversimplified and inadequate definition. Big

Chief Adjuah (née Christian Scott) of the Xodokan (the Brave), grandson of the late Big Chief Donald Harrison Sr. and nephew to Big Chief Donald Harrison Jr. of the Congo Nation, described who and what the Black masking Indians are on his Instagram page as "Louisiana based West African tribal Chiefdoms" that have been "rebelling and liberating themselves since the 1710s." While his caption goes on to discuss the "hybridized," or syncretized, practices of these "maroon" groups that evolved through slavery, Indian removal, and segregation, it lacks an explicit why.

So, who are the Black masking Indians of New Orleans besides a three- to four-dozen-plus cadre of individual families who like to get dressed up and mask in elaborate costumes on Carnival? They are the descendants of New Orleans's enslaved, Indigenous, free people of color, and European populations. Why do they exist? Why do they do what they do? Why are their stories worthy of being told in this book? Those answers can begin to be unfolded in the retelling of their history.

ON THE CONTINENT

The first known contact between Africans and Europeans dates back to the fifteenth century and the Portuguese. With the mission of spreading Christianity through Catholicism, the Portuguese received two separate blessings from two different popes to colonize the Americas and its Native peoples while also authorizing the enslavement of Africans. This holy sanctioning solidified the brutal and barbaric future course of the transatlantic slave trade that was already beginning.

When the Portuguese began to introduce their Catholic customs and practices to African tribes, they started with the people they encountered in South, West, and Central Africa. They also established trading posts, stole land for themselves, and created plantations for the enslaved to work. Jeroen Dewulf notes that when the Portuguese came into contact with the Kingdom of Kongo, in Central Africa (what is made up today of the northwestern portion of Angola and the southwestern part of the modern Democratic Republic of Congo) in 1483, they quickly went about the work to convert the kingdom's monarchy and social elite. That work was completed by 1491. These new converts then set about converting their own people: "[They] were well aware of the fact that the dissemination of Catholicism would fail if it were superimposed on indigenous beliefs. Hence, the new Kongolese faith developed into a profoundly syncretic variant of Catholicism that incorporated indigenous traditions related to curing, healing, and divination."

Dewulf posits that one major conversion tool was the incorporation of Catholicism with other Kongolese rituals and practices, specifically the *sangamento*: "*Sangamento* is derived from the verb ku-sanga in the local Kikongo language and evokes the spectacular leaps, contortions, and gyrations of the dancers." The term *sangamento* was coined by the Portuguese in reference to ritual war dances that were accompanied by a band playing various instruments. The dancers "would typically wear 'a belt . . . with bells attached to it . . . so arranged that when fighting with their enemies the sounds [would] give them courage.'"

The Kongolese *sangamento.* Note the feathers worn on the head and the raffia-like fringe at the waist area of the soldier's skirt. These are similar to today's golden crowns made by Indian gangs and the raffia attachments worn specifically by those who play the Wild Man. Reproduced from Filippo Pigafetta, *Relatione del reame di Congo et delle circonvicine contrade, tratta dalli scritti & ragionamenti di Odoardo Lopez* (1591), courtesy Antiquariaat Forum, Netherlands.

This description of the dancers of the *sangamento* sounds much like a description of a Wild Man or a Spy Boy in today's Mardi Gras Indian tribes, who run blocks ahead of their Big Chief, their suits adorned in bells, to awaken the neighborhood and alert other tribes to their impending presence. These descriptions can also be extrapolated to the meeting of two tribes where members of each position from the Wild Man to the Big Chief compete by doing a ritualistic dance where they show off their suits, agility, masculine or feminine prowess, and overall prettiness in an attempt to signify who bested the other.

There are many evolutionary steps between the *sangamentos* in the Kingdom of Kongo and the Black masking Indians of New Orleans. These steps include the many ways in which the rituals of the Catholic faith were braided together with the rituals of the Kongolese spiritual practices.

Initially, the practice of the Catholic faith included a rich parade tradition where celebrants, devotees, and followers of Christ would march through the streets on important feast days in the liturgical calendar with floats and other bands of merriment. The syncretic variant in the Kingdom of Kongo was easily enfolded into already existing religious structures. Now the Kingdom of Kongo marked important feast days with the aforementioned *sangamentos*. The Portuguese also introduced the concept of Catholic brotherhoods—mutual-aid societies that dedicated a lot of time and attention to burial ceremonies (not unlike some of New Orleans's own social aid and pleasure clubs and benevolent societies as well as the Black masking Indian tribes). The brotherhoods required the election of a king, queen, judge, prince, and count in "election ceremonies [that] were accompanied by parades and dances, where Iberian traditions came to be mixed with indigenous African elements."

This syncretism with the evolution of Catholic brotherhoods and their election ceremonies is also indicative of today's Black masking Indian tribes and how they structure themselves in terms of roles and positions. The evidence in this brief description clearly demonstrates that the culture and traditions of the Old World carried into the New.

IN AMERICA

In America, there was already a unique and distinct Indigenous culture in and around New Orleans, and up and down the Mississippi River, before any Europeans or Africans arrived. This unique culture included styles of dress, dancing, music, worship, language, and more. But piecing this history together into a cohesive, linear story is difficult due to genocide, removal, and erasure. What we are left with, then, to compile a narrative of a people that so influenced our subject, the Black masking Indians of New Orleans, are "only fragmentary traces to go by—mostly in the form of material artifacts such as musical instruments . . . [and] knowledge derived from colonial archives" written and documented from the point of view of the conquerors and colonizers.

To that end, there exist three hundred years of history between Indigenous tribes and Europeans in the lower Mississippi River valley. However, it is important to know that people of African descent make up some of the population of these Indigenous tribes during that history. That is because "people of African descent—'free and enslaved'—were present in North America as early as the 1500s." This sixteenth-century presence in North America includes in the area of the lower Mississippi valley and predates the French naming of the Louisiana colony in 1682, its official founding in 1699 by Pierre Le Moyne d'Iberville, and the establishment of the city of New Orleans in 1718 by the French explorer Jean-Baptiste Le Moyne de Bienville, Iberville's younger brother. During Bienville's explorations of the mouth of the Mississippi River he noted "a Spanish settlement" of "whites, mulattoes and blacks." He also mentioned a large Indigenous village called Connessi, "village of the blacks," where there were only Black families present.

Since the Gulf of Mexico was claimed by Spain, Dewulf offers that the Black families Bienville encountered were runaway slaves who accompanied Spanish explorers on their voyages to the New World. If we assume this to be true, this analysis must go a step further to note that these Black families in community with "whites and mulattoes" were escaped Africans who found solace with the Indigenous communities who already lived near and around the mouth of the Mississippi River. As noted in the 2003 documentary *All on a Mardi Gras Day,* Indigenous tribes had provided refuge to enslaved Africans since the first colonies were established in what became the United States of America. Or as Charles Duvernay, the Spy Boy for the Young Maasai Hunters Tribe, said, "You know, they won't tell you there were already Black Indians here."

Therefore these "Black Indians" were among the populace of the Indigenous tribes in the lower Mississippi valley who first witnessed the arrival of French explorers and settlers during the earliest days of the Louisiana colony in 1682. There were more than two dozen tribes living in the area at the time of the French arrival; numerous tribes lived around the river because it "was both a superhighway and a center of gravity for many families, bands, clans, tribes, and larger linguistic communities." This central force of life led to the creation of a common tongue used among the tribes known as Mobilian Jargon, of which some words are still present in the Black masking Indian lexicon today; a ceremony for greeting known as the calumet, or the so-called peace pipe ceremony; as well as the sharing of musical practices.

The shared musical practices revolved around percussion instruments, namely drums; a gourd-like rattle known as the *chichicois,* a predecessor of the modern tambourine; singing; and dancing. These practices were present in calumet ceremonies. One such ceremony took place shortly after the founding of New Orleans in 1718, known as the "Marche du Calumet de Paix," or Peace Pipe March.

Such a public musical procession would not have been foreign to the French settlers due to their Catholic background and familiarity with Parisian Carnival. It also would not have been foreign to the enslaved Africans who were surely nearby during the ceremony—though their presence was not explicitly documented. Furthermore, these calumet ceremonies and public processions were a way the French settlers introduced themselves to the Indigenous tribes up and down the Mississippi River: "The musical procession in New Orleans in 1718 represented the culmination of the peace settlement after a ruthless war conducted by the French against the Chitimacha that had lasted several years and ended in mass enslavement of the latter, who were the first group in the New Orleans area to suffer this particular kind of calamity on a large scale."

Although these ceremonial introductions were full of merriment and revelry, they were very necessary for maintaining a tenuous peace between the untrusting tribes and the unscrupulous settlers. For example, a peace pipe ceremony was held after "the Natchez had annihilated Fort Rosalie, in late autumn of 1729, when wounded and dazed survivors straggled into the city [of New Orleans] to tell the news that 'all was fire and blood' upriver."

These descriptions of bloody battles and joyful peace ceremonies contradict the often-advanced narrative of the pliant and submissive primitive first encountered by the Europeans in Plymouth that led to the first Thanksgiving. Beyond the American myth of Indigenous peoples, what we find in these descriptions is a people who were fierce in their resistance and only acquiescent to peace on their terms.

Also in these descriptions of peaceful meetings between Indigenous tribes and Europeans are echoes of what can be observed in Black masking Indian culture today. On Mardi Gras Day when masking tribes take to the street, they must decide which tribes they'll meet in ritualistic ceremony and those they won't. During the time of Big Chief Donald Harrison Sr., he would decide whether or not to meet another tribe or even a solo Indian out playing without a tribe for the day based on how they were dressed. Harrison relayed one such story to biographer Al Kennedy about what he would say in those instances: "Don't stop! Just keep going! Just walk over him because he's not dressed like a Chief! Just walk over him!"

Although the circumstances and rules of the rituals Harrison adhered to in the mid-twentieth century were much different from the peace pipe ceremonies Indigenous tribes took part in with Europeans two hundred years earlier, the foundational reason was the same: to establish peace and avoid violence. In the late nineteenth and early twentieth centuries, one tribe "walking over another" could lead to violent clashes between rival Indian gangs on Mardi Gras morning, just as settlers trying to stake out land and a living among Indigenous tribes could lead to violent clashes between the two warring groups in the early days of white settler colonialism in New Orleans. That these signs and ways of respect endure to this day some three hundred years later is indicative of how deeply entrenched the cultural customs of Native groups are in the Black masking Indian tradition, a New Orleans tradition that could not come to be without the intense mixing and cultural exchange of Blacks and Indigenous peoples together.

IN NEW ORLEANS

The first enslaved Africans arrived in New Orleans in 1719, just a year after the city's founding. Their arrival came at a volatile time in the history of the Louisiana colony: "For twenty years or more after its founding in 1699, France's Louisiana colony regularly faced the threat of starvation." This threat forced the newcomers to go and live with the nearby Indigenous communities until they could once again sustain themselves. This practice would continue even after the arrival of the first enslaved Africans, who were brought to turn the seaport into an agricultural center of commerce.

Some of the first enslaved Africans in New Orleans were from the Kingdom of Kongo in Central Africa as well as the Senegambia region on the continent's west coast. "Starting in 1719," writes Dewulf, “the number of African slaves increased rapidly. Records show that, between 1719 and 1743, twenty-three ships brought some 4,000 enslaved people from Senegambia, some 1,750 from the Gulf of Benin, and some 300 from the Kongo region to Louisiana.” Yet the increasing numbers of enslaved laborers did nothing to better the colonists’ chances of survival, even though that’s the bet the planters hedged with themselves: expand the labor force, work the land, increase the profits of both food and money. In fact, the opposite happened. This helped shape the relationship between the enslaved population, the Indigenous tribes, and the white colonizers: “In many cases [the planters] could not even afford to feed their increased number of slaves. To solve the problem, the planters moved to make their slaves more nearly self-sufficient. They began to assign slaves individual parcels of land on which to grow their own food as well as sell their crops.”

This, combined with the fact that the majority of the slaves brought to the colony were male and thus sought out wives who were Indigenous, led to a further intermixing between Indigenous tribes and Africans and generations of free people along with their children. The white colonizers sought out the Indigenous tribes for help when they could not sustain themselves or the ranks of their enslaved, whereas the enslaved Africans sought out these same tribes for refuge and freedom. This common friend—albeit for different reasons—contributed to the unique ethnic and racial makeup of New Orleans. The planters’ insistence on certain freedoms for their slaves also helped to create the *gens de couleur libres,* the largest community of free Blacks in the antebellum South.

These free Blacks may have bought their freedom with the money earned from their trade or the sale of their goods on the weekend. They may have also escaped their plantations and taken refuge with Indigenous tribes as noted in personal ads describing runaway slaves in local newspapers:

> "Louis is more Indian than Negro . . . wears long black hair parted in the centre, and has little or no beard."
>
> "TWENTY FIVE DOLLARS REWARD.—Ran away from David Lanaux's plantation, in St. Charles parish, HENRY, a bright mulatto, five feet six or seven inches high, strongly built, speaking English, French, and the Choctaw dialect. He formerly belonged to Mr. Beauregard, and was employed for some time in the office of the Bee. It is thought that he is in New Orleans, whence he will try to go to the other side of Lake Pontchartrain, or Westward."

As the Louisiana colony shifted hands from French to Spanish to French to American rule, Indigenous tribes managed to secure their autonomy—for a time—after being enslaved, resisting the settlers, helping them survive, and providing refuge for escaped Africans and their descendants who made it to their ranks. This autonomy and freedom came through hard fights that gave the Indigenous tribes—in general and of the lower Mississippi River valley specifically—an esteemed reputation among those held in bondage.

Although they were not seen as remotely equal to the white settlers, their reputation for fighting and the respect they garnered because of it set the Indigenous people in a class that was separate and apart from the intense racial hatred that plagued Black people living under the blight of New Orleans's feudal caste system. For a time the Indigenous tribes lived on the margins, on the periphery of the city, and as yet did not pose an immediate threat or inconvenience to the white settler population: "On the outskirts of New Orleans groups of Houmas, Chitimachas, and Choctaws camped along Bayou St. John and Bayou Road [and in] the city's streets and in the marketplace, Indian women peddled baskets, mats, sifters, plants, herbs, and firewood [while the men] sold venison, wildfowl, and cane blowguns and occasionally earned wages as day laborers and dockworkers."

In short, the tribes were tolerated until an influx of Americans into New Orleans forced a significant change in the multicultural city that had at one time been more accepting of the customs of the people who were there before. The Americans, by contrast, were hostile and domineering, assertive in their ways, rights, and laws that eventually began to erase the Indigenous people from the very streets and squares that had belonged to them for centuries.

The Marshall Trilogy—a series of Supreme Court decisions under Chief Justice John Marshall—which began with *Johnson v. McIntosh* in 1823, effectively stripped Indigenous tribes of their land under its doctrine of discovery. The ruling allowed European Christian settlers to claim land as their own if it was uninhabited by Christians. The violence against Indigenous tribes was exacerbated in 1830, when President Andrew Jackson signed into law the Indian Removal Act, forcing tribes to give up their lands to western-bound settlers and relocate.

As noted by the late Medicine Man and musician Goat Carson in the documentary *Tootie's Last Suit,* Indigenous tribes were forced to make a monumental decision of choosing their innate identity or their home: "You had Indians who were still living in the swamp who suddenly couldn't call themselves Indians. You had Black Indians who could no longer acknowledge their heritage. So you got a lot of Louisiana Indians going as Italians or Cajuns. That's one of the reasons the heritage went underground and took a while to flourish back up because of the oppression from the Indian Removal Act."

Federal laws in addition to Louisiana laws and state court decisions further codified race, identified Indians as people of color, and solidified the one-drop rule to keep Black people in their subservient place, which hastened the vanishing of Native tribes: "Consequently, as the decades passed, there developed an unusually high degree of intermixing of the two groups [Black and Indigenous] and their cultures, an intermixing that, by the end of the nineteenth century, had resulted in the absorption of the local Indian populations into the New Orleans black community."

This absorption was by no means total and complete. Within the Black community, both free and enslaved, there remained key distinctions based on African tribal affiliation and degradations of skin color with differentiations between "negroes," mulattoes, and Creoles. Furthermore, while some Indigenous peoples assimilated into Black culture out of necessity, their own unique culture only added to the cultural tapestry that had been woven with Africans in America since the fifteenth century. The music, the instruments, the goods, the style of dress—especially for Carnival—and the language became syncretized with European and African customs.

No matter the circumstance of their life's lot, free or enslaved, an unbreakable bond was forged between African and Indigenous communities. This bond was an acknowledgment of a common enemy, of individual histories and cultures that existed before that enemy made himself known, and a carrying of that culture to the one place where they could express themselves freely—if only on the weekends, even if it had been tainted, perverted, or syncretized with the culture of their oppressor.

From this syncretism emerged some of the greatest cultural phenomena America gets credit for today, including jazz; the second line; social aid and pleasure clubs; benevolent societies; and, of course, Black masking Indians. All of which was birthed out of the convergence of these three groups (Europeans, Africans, and Indigenous tribes) on one unique marketplace: Congo Square.

THE ENEMY OF MY ENEMY IS MY FRIEND

In Congo Square, enslaved Africans, their Black descendants, the free people of color, and Indigenous tribes all gathered on Sunday afternoons on a small patch of grass to sell their wares, sing, and dance in a pseudofreedom even enjoyed by the white gaze. This bustling marketplace, as it came to be, was born out of the aforementioned struggle of the early days of the Louisiana colony, and the city of New Orleans, where food shortages for the colonists and the enslaved were frequent. After seeking refuge with Indigenous tribes for a time, the colonists who owned slaves granted them a weekend of freedom, in the name of survival.

"Masters give their negroes Saturday and Sunday to themselves, and during that time the master does not give them any food; they then work for other Frenchmen who have no slaves and who pay them," Jean-François Dumont noted in his 1753 memoirs. This practice of the enslaved having free weekends to do as they pleased evolved into the activities of Congo Square that were in full swing by at least the 1740s. In fact, "the trading activities of [the enslaved] had come to form a significant feature of New Orleans's mercantile life, one sufficiently profitable to excite the attention and envy of local retail merchants."

But it was not the entrepreneurial spirit of the enslaved that drew the most attention or even the most ire. It was what was taking place on the square between the people that evolved into the various strands of culture we recognize today—the singing and the dancing. "While African dances had been performed on the Congo Plains, as well as at other locations in the city, and on some plantations since the importation of slaves began in the 1720s," the growth of the Congo Square market expanded the way the square was encountered and gave it a distinct heartbeat and focal point.

Antoine-Simon Le Page du Pratz documented one such gathering in his writings on the Louisiana colony dated from 1718 to 1734. In his *Histoire de la Louisiane,* he noted three to four hundred Blacks who gathered on Sunday "under the pretense of *calinda*" (or of dancing). Such observations were noted by travelers, explorers, visitors, settlers, and newspapers throughout the French and Spanish rule of the Louisiana colony until well into the nineteenth century and the establishment of Louisiana statehood. In 1799 a similar observation was made by an unidentified new white settler, who remarked on the number of Black people singing, dancing, drumming and "fifing" in "large rings" on the levee.

One of the most noted encounters is that of the English engineer Benjamin Henry Latrobe in February 1819. He thought he heard a cavalcade of horses near the rear of the city, or "back-o'-town," when in fact he was hearing "a crowd of 5 or 600 persons assembled in an open space or public square . . . all blacks," with not even a dozen "yellow faces" in the crowd. During this encounter he noted that he saw several "circular groups," "women dancing" while holding the ends of a handkerchief and screaming out one note, dancers moving to the rhythm of the circle's music "hardly moving their feet or bodies," and a song sung "in some African language." These descriptions of Africans holding onto and performing their traditions in the New World—Kongo dances, *sangamentos,* and brotherhood election ceremonies—are similar to the recollections of some Mardi Gras Indians who have traveled to Africa and observed "their culture" there.

"Indians dance on their toes, Africans dance flat-footed just like we dance," Bo Dollis Jr., Big Chief of the Wild Magnolias, said in 2020: "We dance flat-footed. Even with the styles I can say it's kind of the same." Big Chief Brian Harrison Nelson of the Guardians of the Flame discussed the similarity in people and culture between Africa and Blacks in New Orleans in the *All on a Mardi Gras Day* documentary: "I went to Ghana in 1999, and there I saw what we have here in New Orleans—the Mardi Gras Indian tradition. I saw it there. There were also second lines; your umbrellas, brass bands, handkerchiefs, and the exact same second-line dances that we do in New Orleans. They were doing them in Ghana in West Africa."

What is made clear by these eighteenth- and nineteenth-century descriptions of Congo Square, and the twentieth-century travels and observations of today's Black masking Indians to different countries in Africa, is that this tradition comes from the African continent, the cradle of life. The circles and rings of singing and dancing Blacks in Congo Square that Latrobe described are Africans and their descendants in the New World. Further connecting Congo Square participants to their homeland traditions was the organization and separation of each ring or circle of dancers by tribe and region.

In his 1880 memoir, *My Southern Home,* former slave William Wells Brown recalled that those who gathered on the square were from "six different tribes of negroes, named after the section of the country from which they came, and their representatives could be seen on the square, their teeth filed, and their cheeks still bearing tattoo marks." Brown noted the largest group as the "Kraels," or Creoles. He also identified the nations and tribes of the "Minahs," "Congos," "Mandringas," "Gangas," "Hiboas," and "the Foulas, the highest type of the African, with but few representatives." Brown observed that "the Minahs would not dance near the Congos, nor the Mandringas near the Gangas." The tribes that Brown recalled refer to the Minas (from the Gold Coast, present-day Ghana), the Kongolese (from Central Africa), the Mandinkas (from the former Mali Empire in West Africa), and, along with other nations and tribes, the Fulas (a nomadic people from West Africa).

More enlightening still regarding the activities of Congo Square and its surrogate assigns is a gathering recounted by Pierre Forrest in 1831 at a place outside the city, near Lake Pontchartrain, known as "The Camp." He described the scene as "a huge green field on the bank of a lake . . . [each group] having its own flag floating atop a

The Bamboula. An artist's rendering of a dance performed in Congo Square. Note the crowd encircling the dancer. Courtesy of the Louisiana State Museum, New Orleans Jazz Museum Collection.

very tall mast, used as a rallying point . . . [for the] dance." The flags Forrest mentions and the reluctance of the people from the different African nations to dance near each other are akin to the tribalism of today's Mardi Gras Indian culture, specifically of those in the Flag Boy, or Gang Flag, position marking the territory of their tribe by posting their flag at a stop on their route, be it a house or barroom. "Whenever they had a stop the Flag Boy would throw it over the gate, the door, the gateway, whatever, and it would stay there until they come out," said the late, great Big Chief Tootie Montana, of the Yellow Pocahontas, in the *Black Indians of New Orleans* documentary. He added, "Now you wanna get in any trouble, you touch that flag."

Beyond the circles of dancing Blacks partitioned by flags, Forrest also mentioned that several Indian families were present at "the Camp to share these ludicrous pleasures." Although Indian families are mentioned specifically only once in the above accounts, they surely were present for these gathered dances in Congo Square and other remote locales in the back o' town because we know the marketplace is where Indigenous men and women sold goods and meat, which means that "they continued to live in New Orleans and the surrounding region." Further illustrating the syncretizing of cultures between the Africans and their descendants and the Indigenous tribes is that "Congo Square is the first place where it is historically recorded that Black people are wearing feathers."

That record of history comes from the Swiss visitor Johann Buechler, who in 1817 described male dancers "in oriental and Indian dress with a Turkish turban of various colors, red, blue, yellow, green and brown with cloths of the same sort around their body to cover their nakedness, because they don't wear any clothes underneath." He also noted that it was "curious" to see Black people "dressed in such a way" as they danced on a Sunday afternoon in the open square behind the city, "[making] the most wonderful bending gestures with their bodies and knees."

From these accounts we can place Indigenous tribes and Black people in and around Congo Square at the same time making music, dancing, and singing. Although this was a "by-product of the square's market function," it remains part of the enduring legacy of Congo

Square, the various cultures that arose out of the square, and Black people of New Orleans. The activities of Congo Square are an anomaly in the American South, which makes the cultures that arose there like jazz and Black masking Indians even more unique. The enslaved population having a degree of autonomy and being allowed to freely mingle with the free populations of Indigenous tribes and the *gens de couleur libres*—especially with some of them being related—"with little or no supervision" is a concept and a "practice [that] never prevailed anywhere [else] in the rest of the [American] South."

This unusual practice became a lightning rod of controversy for the American newcomers who flooded into Louisiana, and New Orleans specifically, after the Louisiana Purchase in 1803. Never in the history of their understanding of chattel slavery had a Black population—enslaved or free—been so empowered to do with their time what they saw fit without the express permission of the white ruling and enslaving class. This difference in the treatment of the enslaved only added to the cultural differences between the white populations: Protestant Anglo-Americans versus the Catholic French and Spanish. As Jerah Johnson wrote in *Congo Square in New Orleans:* "While the city, during its long colonial history, had accommodated a number of other incoming cultural groups—the Indians, the Africans, some Germans, and a few Spaniards—it had never had to deal with anything like the numbers, assertiveness, determination, or sheer foreignness represented by the American invasion."

This invasive cultural clash resulted in the Americans trying to assert themselves over the common customs that had persisted in New Orleans since its founding. This assertion was a show of conquering dominance, based on racism, classism, and white supremacy, and displayed during one of the city's greatest celebratory feats—Mardi Gras.

Believing that the attitude of the French and Spanish toward the enslaved and free Blacks was too laissez-faire, the Americans showed their power and strength by inciting fear in a city where the Black/African population overwhelmingly outnumbered its white, ruling, elite class. Even though the ruling class maintained their grip on power through cruel public displays of horror such as lynchings and executions, the traditions of the Black/African and Indigenous tribes were too codified, too ritualized, and too common to be eradicated from the people's lives. The rituals from their homeland and mother culture—even perverted with Catholicism of some kind—proved inextinguishable and are maintained to this day in a masking mockery of those who tried to take it away.

THE MASK AND THE MARDI GRAS

Mardi Gras has been celebrated in New Orleans since early in its establishment, and Indians and Black people have been present in the festivities—either as participants or as masked characters—for just as long. One of the earliest accounts of these cultures coming together is in a 1730 Lundi Gras account from the memoir of French explorer Marc-Antoine Caillot. With eleven people in the masking party, Caillot described how he convinced his friends to ultimately participate and the identities they assumed for the occasion: "Some were in red clothing, as Amazons, others in clothes trimmed with a braid, others as women . . . accompanied by eight actual Negro slaves, who each carried a flambeau to light our way."

This early account was recorded during the French rule of New Orleans. However, even during the nearly forty-year Spanish rule of the city, French Mardi Gras customs and traditions did not die out. During this time Carnival activities such as masking were regulated with the goal of controlling the activities of the Black population, who continued to have more free rein and control over their bodies and whereabouts than did Black people elsewhere in the American South. Specifically, colonial documents suggest banning feathers as a disguise and refer to Blacks—free and enslaved—who used the Carnival season to pass through the streets and get into dance halls or even plot rebellions against their white masters. Although the regulations did not extend to white Mardi Gras revelers, the race-based suspicion surrounding the activities of Black Mardi Gras celebrants led to a simmering culture clash where those in power waited for any excuse, no matter how insignificant, to assert their authority. Such was the case when, after the Louisiana Purchase, the American governor W. C. C. Claiborne suspended Carnival in 1806 after receiving word of a possible military coup.

Mardi Gras did not make a resurgence in the city until 1823 due to "ill-feeling between Creoles and Americans," "a racial situation," and "Americans never [approving] of Mardi Gras" in the first place, as Robert Tallant noted in his book *Mardi Gras . . . As It Was.* But when Mardi Gras came back, the Blacks and the Indians participated in the festivities as if they had never been banned.

During the 1823 Carnival season, a visiting Protestant minister described Blacks participating in a Carnival procession behind a "king" wearing "oblong, gilt-paper boxes on his head, tapering upwards, like a pyramid." There were also "characters" following him in their own "peculiar dress and their own contortions," as well as "moody and silent sons of the forest," assumed to be actual Indigenous people, all participating in the dancing, singing, and music making required of the procession.

This description mirrors the brotherhood election ceremonies and other syncretized Catholic/African rituals performed in the Kingdom of Kongo. It is also a prescient nod to today's Black masking Indian tribes when they emerge in the earliest hours of daylight, each man or woman making their own call and doing their own dance according to their rank and position in the tribe.

That actual Indigenous tribes were following the Black maskers and participating in the celebration in their own way in the 1823 scene only gives more credence to the fact that several distinct cultures syncretized into one. It also highlights the venerable significance of Congo Square—the place where these cultures were allowed to mix and marry—as the birthplace of Black Mardi Gras cultural customs that are still exhibited and practiced to this day. Finally, this 1823 encounter is especially significant because just seven years after Black maskers and "sons of the forest" were observed celebrating together, the Indian Removal Act was signed into law, driving Indigenous groups underground and to the margins of culture out of safety and necessity. That the Indians remained on the fringes of culture despite "continued cultural overlaps with people of African descent" validates the part of the origin story of the Mardi Gras Indians that suggests that the masking took place as an homage to Indigenous tribes.

While there are many accounts of Carnival activities continuing from 1823 on, including the addition of a large concluding parade beginning in 1830 to end the season that runs from Three Kings Day to Fat Tuesday, it is worthwhile to note, during this period in American history, especially in the 1840s and 1850s, the growing tensions between the North and South that ultimately led to the fracturing of the country and the Civil War. It was at this time that modern Carnival and Mardi Gras as we know it emerged, perhaps for two different reasons: a change in Catholic customs and American racism and white supremacy.

The Catholic Church began to become more conservative in its celebration of major feast days of the liturgical calendar in response to the Reformation by the newly formed Protestant denominations in the late seventeenth century. As a part of these changes, "theatrical rituals involving dancing in Catholic processions . . . were gradually separated from the actual procession and later banned altogether." This ban left a willing body politic of faithful African-descended believers who were also theatrical performers with their own performance rituals, practices, and customs, and who were without an outlet to showcase their history, legacy, and ancestry.

The removal of the Catholic Church's approval of these processional celebrations during major feast days did not stop celebrants from participating and organizing their own processions during Carnival. Adherence to the conservatism of the changing Catholic Church may have been less influential in how Carnival in New Orleans was shaped.

In New Orleans, the role of racialized hatred and white supremacy served as a leading determinant in how modern Mardi Gras came to be celebrated. Americans who infiltrated New Orleans after the Louisiana Purchase hated the freedoms of the Black population, especially on Carnival day. They hated the ways of the French and Spanish, the latter who allowed Parisian Carnival customs to continue during their reign, and the former who started them in the first place. However, this abhorrence of the customs and cultures of the colony they bought did nothing to eradicate that culture, no matter how harshly it was regulated even though that regulation was never turned on white revelers. In an effort to assert political authority and impose a racial hierarchy in the city, invitation-only secret societies were formed that were anti-Black, anti-Semitic, and akin to the KKK. As author James Gill noted in the documentary *Tootie's Last Suit,* there is "no question that the origin of the modern Carnival is Confederate."

The first modern Mardi Gras Krewe formed from this racist origin was the Mistick Krewe of Comus, established in 1856. Comus and its formalized parade were an attempt by the Anglo-Americans who formed the krewe "to prove that [they were] not just better in administrating the city but even in organizing public celebrations." These celebrations also restored the racialized order limiting Black participants in Mardi Gras to subservient roles, such as carrying flambeaux to light the way for the Comus krewe as they did in the aforementioned account from the 1730 Lundi Gras. But while the formation of Comus may have limited the Black population in their parade and celebration of Mardi Gras, it did nothing to curtail or stop the Carnival celebrations among the Black and remaining Indigenous communities in the back o' town.

English journalist George Sala observed in 1864 that the "Negroes have gone extensively into masquerading on their own private account [and] have been capering about the streets." In 1864, in the midst of the Civil War, Black people were masking for Mardi Gras. We know that Indians, as a character, had remained popular as a Mardi Gras costume since the eighteenth century, and that Indigenous tribes participated in Carnival, even if only from the outskirts. Given this knowledge, it is worth posing the question, as did Lief and McCusker, of when exactly did today's Mardi Gras Indian tribes as we know them first emerge. The oft-quoted date of 1886 with Big Chief Becate Baptiste of the Creole Wild West is puzzling, as Baptiste was only thirteen years old that year.

Lief and McCusker suggest that it was the generation of Becate's father, Jean Baptiste Eugene, who first brought out the Mardi Gras Indian tribes that we know today. Eugene is noted for serving in the Corps d'Afrique during the Civil War along with Samuel Jerry and Henry Horton, both of whose sons were arrested in 1895 in Algiers after a fight broke out between masked Indians on Mardi Gras Day. The *Daily Picayune* of New Orleans wrote: "At 3 p.m. yesterday Algiers was imperiled by what appeared to be a band of hostile Indians. Much consternation was caused when this intrepid band of red men made their debut . . . On closer examination the Indians were discovered to be colored men, who gave their names as follows: Joe Horton, Hy. Jerry, Harry Conners, Henry Lean, Eddie McKinley, John Smith, R. J. Jones, and Walter Brown."

Of that group, John Smith and Walter Brown were only about twenty-one at the time of their arrest in 1895, which means they would have been twelve at the time of the emergence of the first tribes in 1886 if that date is to be upheld. Henry Jerry and Joe Horton, whose fathers also served in the Corps d'Afrique, would have been twenty-six and twenty-eight in 1895 and seventeen and nineteen in 1886. The oldest of those arrested was Henry Lean at age fifty-eight. Although it is not unlikely that the younger men of the group masked in 1886, it *is* unlikely that they formulated and led groups of grown men as masked Black Indians in a tradition that is conditioned upon rank and respect.

There is a long history, recollection, and record of people masked as Indians during Mardi Gras, be they Black, white, or actual Indigenous members themselves. In 1846, Englishman Charles Lyell witnessed some "Indians with feathers in their heads." In 1854 "a party of Indians in full costume" was a notable sighting, along with the scene of a "wild Indian" in 1855. The popularity of the Indian character, despite the United States' oppressive policies toward the people, never waned. Their resurgence in nineteenth-century pop culture is attributed to the Wild West shows that started as early as 1843. In these shows the Indians—plains tribes and not bayou nations—were characterized as strong, beautiful, and defiant; they were remembered and celebrated for the very characteristics that led to their genocide and removal. The Black population, however, was never allowed to show these characteristics or to assert agency over their own personhood.

By 1870, the Indian had become so common as a Mardi Gras character that they are documented alone and in groups and caught up in the judicial system. An encounter a year later recorded in the New Orleans *Times-Democrat,* however, is even more notable: "Among the revelers we observed a tall and graceful Indian, his hirsute adornment trading [*sic*] the ground after the manner of the chief described in Catlin's painting. We saluted him with a few familiar Choctaw words, and as 'ye gentle savage,' it was his duty to have replied as becomes the denizen of the woody wilds. But he spake never a word, not comprehending the meaning of our words of recognition or salutation. What business had he dressing a character he could not play?"

This masked Indian who did not respond in Choctaw could have easily been a masked Black man who did not fully know the Mobilian Jargon language save for a few words and phrases that remain in the Mardi Gras Indian lexicon today, including "bamboula" and "jockomo feena ne." Bamboula is the beat contemporary Mardi Gras Indians say is the foundation for all of their music and songs. However, Lief and McCusker posit that "bamboula" was derived from Mobilian Jargon *babela* but conflated with the famous dance associated with Congo Square and the musical composition by Louis Moreau Gottschalk. As for "jockomo feena ne," the famed lyric from the song "Iko, Iko," it is believed to be derived from the Choctaw term "achukma," which means "good," and the phrase "achukmafehna," meaning "very good." One of its early usages is heard in the description of a Mardi Gras celebration in 1879: "Every face looks like a mask, and every dress like a fantastic costume. 'Huzza! Here's one of 'em. Chick-a-ma-feeno! Chick-a-ma-feeno!,' they shout as an Indian makes his way through the crowd jingling his bells and flourishing his tomahawk."

Although it is not explicitly stated that the Indian in the above account is a masked Black man, we cannot be certain that he is not, especially with the overwhelming evidence that Black people masked on Mardi Gras throughout the nineteenth century and that Indians were on the street and widely accepted at Mardi Gras, either in person or as a costume, just four decades after their forcible removal.

This collision course of American hatred with the racist formations of "The Mistick Krewe of Comus, Twelfth Night Revelers, Rex, Momus, and others" along with the resurgence of the Indian as a star set the backdrop for the emergence of the Mardi Gras Indian tribes as we know them ten to possibly twenty years before the often-cited start date of 1886. That means they formed out of the ashes of the Civil War during the period of Reconstruction, when America achieved an enforced racial parity. That parity would not last as the bitter remnants of the Confederacy rose again just a decade later.

At the end of Reconstruction, white supremacy emerged in the form of Jim Crow. Separate but equal was the law of the South even during Carnival in New Orleans. Only one other group could innately identify with the oppression of Black people in New Orleans, and those were the Indigenous people who had been removed or gone underground decades earlier. Only now they were enjoying a peak in their popularity thanks to the Wild West shows, including that of Buffalo Bill, who came to the city during the World's Industrial and Centennial Cotton Exposition from 1884 to 1885. This show is often cited as the underpinning of the origins of the Mardi Gras Indians, but this legend is only partially true.

The dancing, singing, processions, and intricately beaded suits that make up the culture of Black masking Indians are distinctly rooted in African, Indigenous, Catholic, and European customs. These customs were present in New Orleans from the time of its inception.

That Anglo-Americans were avidly consuming Indigenous culture through their attendance at Wild West shows by the end of the nineteenth century provided an outlet for both natural-born members of Indigenous tribes as well as Black Carnival celebrants to showcase their culture without fear of repercussion. It was a mask of a mask meant to mock white supremacy, Rex, and segregation, all while showing off what it means to be proud, strong, and defiant.

This stance was solidified in the meaning of the sacred Mardi Gras Indian song "Indian Red." The song opens with a Big Chief shout-singing "Madi cu defio," a phrase Dewulf believes originates from the French "Mallé couri dan déser." In his translation of the lyrics and the possible original French, Dewulf finds a connection between "cu defio" and the word *sangamento* that would give the opening of the song a meaning that roughly says, "Who is there to stop me from organizing a *sanga* war dance at this plantation and getting the support from the whole of Louisiana?" That the song continues in English with the lyrics, "We won't bow down / Not on the ground / The Indians of the Nation / The Whole Wide Creation / I love to hear them call my Indian Red," further reinforces the defiant spirit of Black masking Indians who formally emerged in New Orleans culture protesting injustice and oppression while also celebrating their long, deep history that reaches back to the time before white men invaded and encroached on Africa and the New World.

In this way, the Mardi Gras Indians were first "a carnivalesque smokescreen" that allowed Black warriors and kings to parade with weapons without raising suspicion within the existing social order. But in this smoke screen they were also fully themselves—fully African and fully Indigenous; they were the descendants of those early intermixing connections, the reason why many Blacks from the region are now prone to say, "I got Indian in my family."

Beyond a way to cast off the negative connotations associated with Blackness, masking is also an unintended embrace of a cultural legacy that remains present and active to this day. Black masking Indians, in taking on the spirit of Indigenous tribes while also honoring African heritage, are proof positive that "African culture in the New World did not die, nor was it lost or destroyed. It was transformed. Like the various European cultures transplanted to these shores, the many African cultures joined and blended with each other and with European and the native American Indian cultures to become a new meld." This new meld became one of the most beautiful and unique yearly phenomena exhibited each Carnival season in New Orleans, the Mardi Gras Indians. These are their stories.

2

Mardi Gras Indians Today

INITIATION

For the uninitiated, the process of becoming a Black masking Indian during Carnival season, and a few occasions beyond, may seem shrouded in mystique. For the many who mask, however, the action step from being a part of the second line following the culture to becoming the culture's main attraction is one propagated by birth or proximity. Allison "Tootie" Montana was born into the culture. The same goes for our interview subjects Bo Dollis Jr., Romeo Bougere, Cherice Harrison Nelson, Keelian Boyd, and Stafford Agee. Others, however, like the late Big Chiefs Donald Harrison Sr. and Robbe Lee, along with interviewees Ronnel Butler, Charles Duvernay, and Gilbert "Cosmo" Dave, grew up with an awareness of the culture and eventually became a part of it due to the proximity of their neighborhood or familial connections to the center of Indian activity.

In chapter 1, I presented Lief and McCusker's theory that the most famous nineteenth-century Indian, "Becate" Baptiste Eugene, probably first masked Indian with and under his father, Jean Baptiste

Eugene, since he was only thirteen years old when he is credited with creating and serving as Big Chief of the Creole Wild West. Even for Becate, masking Indian was part of his family birthright. This same birthright was passed on to one of the most famous Mardi Gras Indians of all, the late Allison "Tootie" Montana.

"My Daddy, according to my mother, my Daddy had [an] uncle that used to mask with her uncle, Becate. Becate Baptiste," Montana said in his aged, gravel-rough voice, as he explained his lineage in the culture in the documentary film *Tootie's Last Suit.* "As far back as anybody living could remember, he was the first Chief. That's right. And he was what? He was Creole. I'm Creole. And that's why the tribe was called Creole Wild West."

Montana, who was born in 1922, came of age in the Indian tradition around the time of two other great chiefs: Donald Harrison and Robert Nathaniel Lee, better known as Big Chief Robbe.

Born in 1915, Big Chief Robbe said he first felt the call to be an Indian on Carnival Day in 1923 when he was eight years old and saw a bunch of men in feathers rush past his house. "I just knew I was going to mask after that," Robbe told biographer Al Kennedy. From that moment on, Robbe said, he looked for and found older men who masked Indian wherever he could until he finally came into contact with the legendary Indian Cornelius "Brother" Tillman.

Brother Tillman was born just before the turn of the century, in 1898. He came from a family that masked Indian, as his uncle, Robert Sam Tillman (1871–1898), was remembered as a leader in the Creole Wild West despite his brutal murder.

Robbe first saw Tillman mask Indian as the second Spy Boy for the Wild Squatoolas sometime in the mid-1920s. When he found out where Tillman lived, he would go around and help the young Indian sew, wrap feathers, and make crowns for his suits. Robbe studied the craft and absorbed the culture from those who lived it, but it wasn't until 1928 that he worked up the courage to ask Brother Tillman, who by then was the Big Chief of the Creole Wild West, if he could mask with him at Mardi Gras the next year. In 1929, at the age of thirteen, Robbe made his debut masking Indian in the Creole Wild West in his own suit of beads and feathers he sewed himself out of rags from the neighborhood ragman, material found in the junkyard, and pins and earrings from girls who couldn't find the match.

Similar to Robbe, the late Big Chief Donald Harrison fell in love with the masked Indians from afar. At three years old, in 1936, he first saw Wild Man Herman of the Creole Wild West. A year later Herman plucked the four-year-old Donald from his porch on Jackson Avenue and told him not to be afraid. From that moment on, Harrison knew he wanted to mask. Twelve years passed between the time Donald Harrison knew he wanted to don the feathers of Indians and the time he finally asked Big Chief Lawrence Fletcher of the White Eagles if he could mask with him in 1949, when he was sixteen years old. This is despite the fact that two of Harrison's uncles, Joseph King and James "Foxy" King, had masked as Mardi Gras Indians early in their lifetimes.

The hesitancy of some parents early in the twentieth century to allow their children, even their older teenaged sons, to mask Indian had to do with the negative reputation of the Mardi Gras Indians at the time—a reputation steeped in brutality, violence, and even murder.

THE VIOLENT PAST

The cultural foundation of the Mardi Gras Indians is a warrior culture. Be it the *sangamentos*—war dances—of the Kongolese and other African tribes brought to New Orleans during the transatlantic slave trade, or the wars waged between the Indigenous tribes and the Europeans over land and territory in the New World, the same resistant and rebellious spirit is fused into the very DNA of Black masking Indians. Born out of the dueling oppressive eras of antebellum slavery and the Indian Removal Act, these fights, skirmishes, and humbugs were fought for seemingly innocuous reasons: small slights, instances of disrespect and insolence, or utter dislike. It is no different than today's much-maligned gang wars in inner cities across the country. Wars that start over turf and territory—be it a block or street corner—can ramp up into full-scale assaults between rival gangs over an area in the neighborhood, disrespect, insolence, or the scuff on a new pair of white shoes. The only difference between the notorious violence of gangs like Los Angeles's Crips & Bloods or Chicago's Gangster Disciples and the early twentieth-century violence between rival gangs of Indians is that the latter group fought while wearing suits of beads and feathers that weighed one hundred pounds or more.

In the 1895 *Daily Picayune* story recounted in chapter 1 where we're first introduced to some of the nineteenth-century Indians, we also find out why they were all named and written about in the first place. It was because they were arrested: "Much consternation was caused when this intrepid band of red men made their debut, but soon the pulses of spectators resumed their normal beat. Ere many minutes elapsed, and while making the rounds, the band became entangled with some white maskers, and a fight ensued, which resulted in the arrest of the whilom Indians, and their confinement in the dark recesses of a special cell in the Eighth precinct station."

Five years later another report, this one in the *Times-Democrat,* detailed the violent happenings between Indians on Mardi Gras:

> Every Mardi Gras bunches of negroes get together masked as Indians and a hundred-strong race through the streets playing fool antics and at the same time have their eyes open for trouble. They always find it when they clash with another organization of their kind and usually there is a free for all fight when they meet.
>
> It was so yesterday when the Red, White and Blue and the Chickasaws met in the afternoon at the corner of Perdido and Franklin streets and as a result two blacks are wounded and three of the Indians are in custody . . . The Red, White and Blues were jealous and some black buck cracked one of the Chickasaws on the head. That started the fight and in a few seconds, everybody was clubbing around, and it looked as though the street would be flooded with coon blood. The negroes got out their pistols and the big blacks were bolting into houses and through windows and falling into the quarters.

At this point in 1900, seeing Black men masked as Indians on Mardi Gras Day was normal, as indicated by the first line of the article, "Every Mardi Gras bunches of negroes get together masked as Indians." Even the shock of the violence between the two clashing tribes is unremarkable. While more details are provided in this write-up than in the snippet of information in the 1895 story, what is clear in the account is that the journalists of the time were no longer unfamiliar with the tradition of Black men masked as Indians, or their violent encounters with one another.

Twenty-three years later, when the Indians rushed past Robbe's gate, inciting his interest in the peculiar culture, it was because of a fight. The *Times-Picayune* headline from February 13, 1923, proclaimed, "Negro Indians Go on Warpath." The paper detailed several different fights that broke out. It all started at Annunciation and Valence when a young girl was hit by a bullet. The police broke up the first fight, but it started up again "across St. Charles Avenue three blocks from Robbe's home at 3006 South Rampart (Danneel)." The fight then continued and finally ended at Louisiana Avenue and Dryades Street. While the paper said the fight involved only two Indian gangs, Robbe told biographer Al Kennedy that he was told there were four tribes involved: Creole Wild West and the Yellow Pocahontas (whose rivalry goes back to the nineteenth century), along with the Wild Squatoolas, and Red, White, and Blue.

These humbugs, as the elder statesmen of the Indian tribes call them, are an extension of the same tribalism first witnessed in Congo Square that William Wells Brown reported on in his memoir. Gone are the names of the African tribes associated with the different rings of people grouped on the square. In their stead are the names of fictional Indian tribes, since the oppression Black people faced in the post-Reconstruction, Jim Crow South forced them to cloak their homage to African heritage behind Indigenous names. The hierarchy, ranking, and respectability politics of African and Indigenous tribalism, however, remained in effect.

No parent, especially no Black mother, in their right mind would willingly allow their children to enter into a culture so closely aligned with violence, no matter how beautiful, engaging, enchanted, and extravagant the processional songs and dances that preceded the violence. Gilbert "Cosmo" Dave wanted to mask Indian ever since he was a small child growing up in the Lower Ninth Ward in the mid-1950s. But his mother wouldn't let him. Standing in one of the exhibition rooms of the House of Dance and Feathers museum, he said, "She wouldn't let me mask at first because I was too young." Mimicking her, he said, "Wait 'til you make eighteen and then you'll be an Indian." Begrudgingly, Dave continued to wait to mask Indian, all the while immersing himself in the culture and sewing suits for his friends and other members in various gangs.

The story is the same for children born into the culture whose fathers, uncles, and older brothers masked. Bo Dollis Jr., born in 1981 to the legendary late Big Chief Bo Dollis Sr. of the Wild Magnolias, recalled that he wasn't supposed to mask Indian despite his father's status in the tradition. Sitting in the living room of his New Orleans East townhouse, his massive, all-white 2020 Indian suit sparkling as it stood sentinel behind him, he said: "My mom was so scared of Indians because back then Indians was more violent. Back in the 60s and 70s they was really cutting each other, stabbing each other, hitting each other with hatchets and stuff like that."

Cara Harrison, the daughter of Big Chief Donald Harrison Sr., told biographer Al Kennedy that she pulled her twin sons from the Indian tradition with their grandfather and uncle, Donald Harrison Jr., because of a shooting that took place at a Sunday parade in the early

1990s: "I wanted them to have the experience of doing it, but there is an element of danger there sometimes with the other gangs, and there are some things you just can't protect your children from . . . If a bullet comes this way I can't protect them from it."

However, the call to mask Indian is greater, deeper, and more intrinsically felt than any parent's forbidding. So on Mardi Gras Day, the wives and mothers would pray for their men and boys as they headed out the door in their colorful suits. "You know mamas used to cry back then," Bo Dollis Jr. said, "because they didn't know if they child was coming back home." Yvonne Harrison, sister to Donald Harrison Sr., recalled that their mother was always fearful when teenaged Donald began masking Indian—afraid that Donald would get "hurt" or "killed." Yvonne's fear was warranted because at that time she recalled the Indians carrying "hatchets" and fighting in an area called the "Bucket of Blood" on "Third and South Rocheblave, . . . [where] the two Indian tribes would meet, and . . . they would war."

Although this history and penchant for violence between Mardi Gras Indian tribes didn't lessen participants' desire, and even need, to mask, it did make them more aware of their own mortality. It also explains why even to this day the tribes recite the Lord's Prayer over themselves after singing "Indian Red" and before heading out for the day's festivities. Jazz bassist Peter Badie, who recalled seeing Indians battle on the Claiborne Avenue neutral ground (before the I-10 overpass was erected) in the 1930s and 1940s, told biographer Al Kennedy, "They never go to church, but they ask their God to protect them during the day." With the prayer and the singing of the ancient hymn, the Indians put their faith and hope in a safe return. Sometimes they returned; sometimes they did not. For the ones who did not make it home, "Indian Red" would be sung over their fallen bodies by passing Indians and tribes, ushering the fallen tribe member to a heavenly home.

"In the past, if a fellow wasn't rough, he didn't mask," said Big Chief Robbe to biographer Al Kennedy, "because he didn't know when something was going to happen." Something like being forced to bow down (a sign of respect when commanded by your Chief) by a rival Indian at pistol-point, a story recounted by Robbe in his biography and that of Donald Harrison. As it happened, a man named Jesse made a man named Albert bow down, saying, "If you don't bow down, your mother and aunt and family are going to see you get shot." Robbe said that though Albert may have been a better a man than Jesse, "he wasn't a better man than that pistol."

Stories like the aforementioned of the violence between Mardi Gras Indians do not stand alone; skirmishes and violence abound to this day. Be it between uptown Indians and downtown Indians—delineated by the style in which they choose to mask (beaded flat patches versus 3D creative arts)—or personal slights held over until Mardi Gras, where the mask makes it harder for perpetrators to be identified, tribe members are always prepared.

In the more distant past they were armed with actual weapons. Tootie Montana said: "They used to carry real shotguns and hatchets. Real hatchets and have them decorated, you know, and they carry they flag on the rod . . . and it was needle-sharp man and they carry they flag on that." The iron rod that was "needle-sharp" was purposely sharpened by a blacksmith, Big Chief Robbe recalled: "I mean, he'd have it so you could stick it up in the pavement. Then he'd bring it home and decorate it. And that was his weapon." Big Chief Drew (Andrew Justin) remembered seeing "a guy get hit in the head with a hatchet" in the late 1940s. He said the Indians used to "fight, shoot, [and] cut."

Despite the frequent occurrences of violence first documented in the late 1800s, calls for peace began as early as the 1930s. The potential peace deal was brokered on the agreement that Indian tribes no longer sing the infamous song "Iko, Iko," with a title the Indian tribes take to mean "kiss my ass" despite the very different etymology from Mobilian Jargon. As one man named Henri told Brother Tillman around 1933, "It's a good song, but it's trouble because the most fellows that can throw the most slangs can make the most trouble."

"Iko, Iko" is not the only song Indians use to throw slang at a rival tribe boasting about their costumes, prowess, and overall strength. In the Maurice Martinez documentary *Black Indians of New Orleans,* the Big Chief of the White Eagles in the mid-1970s is throwing slang to the song "Shallow Water," and in his improvised lyrics it is evident that he is very aware of the danger that faces him on the street as he meets the various tribes.

(Shallow Water Oh Mama)
We gon' meet everybody, gon' turn around
(Shallow Water Oh Mama)
I'm pretty a White Eagle, I'm going uptown
(Shallow Water Oh Mama)
I told my mama and my little bitty wife

(Shallow Water Oh Mama)
I'm a mask this year if it cost my life
(Shallow Water Oh Mama)
On Mardi Gras morning don't weep and moan
(Shallow Water Oh Mama)
We the pretty White Eagles when we leave home
(Shallow Water Oh Mama)
I told my brothers, said get out of town
(Shallow Water Oh Mama)
We the pretty White Eagles and there they come
(Shallow Water Oh Mama)
The pretty White Eagles that don't look down
(Shallow Water Oh Mama) . . .

Another version of "Shallow Water" that Al Kennedy recorded from Donald Harrison Sr. included the lines:

I'll shoot my pistol on a Mardi Gras Day
I'll make scary Indians get the hell out my way

These lyrics are equally as incendiary as those of "Iko, Iko," with its verse that goes:

My Spy Boy told your Spy Boy
Sitting on the bayou,
My Spy Boy told your Spy Boy
I'm a set your ass on fire

Or the version Tootie Montana sang with Kenneth A. Lewis, the Wild Man of the Mandingo Warriors, in the Circle Foods parking lot:

> Your Spy Boy eat raw pork chop
> My Spy Boy eat liver
> Mess with us on a Mardi Gras Day
> We gonna run your ass in the river

These songs and their lyrics are all indicative of the warrior culture of the Mardi Gras Indians, whose members may be set off into a fit of violence by any perceived slight or by feelings of jealousy.

Indians from many tribes tried for decades to broker peace between rival gangs. Although it always proved to be tenuous and temporary, it was this foundational work that laid the path for Big Chiefs Donald Harrison Sr., Tootie Montana, Bo Dollis Sr., and several others to achieve overall peace between the tribes when they decided that Indians would no longer fight with their fists, hatchets, guns, and other weaponry but rather with their artistry.

KILL 'EM DEAD WITH NEEDLE AND THREAD

In July 2020, in the midst of a global pandemic that ravaged New Orleans after the city held Mardi Gras on February 25 because the severe threat of the novel coronavirus that caused the COVID-19 infection had not been clearly communicated, I visited the homes of several men and women who participate in the Mardi Gras Indian tradition. Inside each home, large or small, I always encountered a massive Indian suit and a small card table or TV tray that held the makings of a new suit.

In the case of every Indian I spoke with, every biography I've read, and every documentary I've watched, the members of the Black masking tradition have all acknowledged that they make a new suit every year, no matter how much it costs them. And to be clear, those costs are more than financial. While coping with the financial strain is definitely part of what it takes to keep this tradition going year after year, the sacrifices these men and women make to keep the culture going take a toll on their body, their health, and their interpersonal relationships. Yet none of them, dead or alive, has wanted to give it up. They do it for the love of the culture, the beauty of the work of their hands, and for the communities and their denizens that have embraced them and look forward to seeing them year after year.

No matter how painstaking the task of sewing tiny beads onto canvas or cardboard, wrapping feathers, or constructing a crown, these Indians, these men and women, combine the skills of an artist, architect, and physicist to make sure that when they step out on the street on Mardi Gras Day, they are the undisputed prettiest. That journey to being pretty begins with learning the craft and sometimes recruiting help along the way.

"My mama had this one purse that had nothing but beads on it," Bo Dollis Jr. said as he detailed how he began to make his first Indian suit at about age eight or nine despite his mother's objections. "She never wore the purse. I could be real honest," he swore. "I never saw my mama wear this purse. And I cut it because I wanted the beads off it." Bo said when his mother finally went looking for the purse and found that he cut it, she agreed to let him mask just the one time as long as he did his chores and kept his grades up. He said, "Well one year led to thirty-something years now." After thirty years of masking Bo is now passing the tradition on to his daughter, whom he observed at just two years old with a needle between her teeth trying to teach herself how to sew.

Bo Dollis Jr.'s artistry and dedication to the craft are shared by many Black masking Indians, but those qualities are often first attributed to Tootie Montana, who was instrumental in brokering peace between the tribes and creating suits the streets of New Orleans had never seen before. Montana credits the construction design of his suits to his trade as a lather. He said he used that knowledge to create his Indian suits because he wasn't taught how when he first started masking with his father. "The year I masked with him, the last year he masked, was the first year I masked," Montana said in the *Black Indians of New Orleans* documentary. In the documentary about his final year making a suit, Montana said, "My Daddy was great in his way, but he never made the stuff that I've made."

In his voice are pride and hubris at the fifty suit creations he'd constructed in his lifetime that he learned how to make on his own without help, guidance, or input from his father. This was a lesson Tootie apparently passed down to his son Darryl. "My Daddy, he never just sat me down and said, 'this is how you do it,'" Darryl proclaimed in the documentary. "I just would sit around the table and watch. He had a whole bunch of little patterns he had drawn. At that time I really couldn't draw. And I found a piece that I thought I wanted to use, and

I took that piece, and I made all the pieces for my apron, made all my pieces for my crown, and that was my suit."

Darryl's introduction and beginnings in the masking tradition came from watching and observing, as did Bo Dollis Jr.'s. However, Romeo Bougere, who began masking Indian at the age of four under his father, the late Big Chief Rudy Bougere Sr. of the 9th Ward Hunters, said the culture ruined and saved his life at the same time, and it all started in his childhood. "He wanted me to follow his steps so bad I didn't go to prom. I didn't get a chance to go outside," Romeo said sitting in his living room in his colorful house on Lamanche in the Lower Ninth Ward. Romeo, in addition to serving as Big Chief of the 9th Ward Hunters, is also a musician. Using the bamboula beat of Indian music as his foundation, he has recorded two albums with fellow Big Chief Jermaine Bossier of the 7th Ward Creole Hunters. As Romeo described his childhood and what it was like growing up masking with his father, he began singing, in a smooth tenor with a distinctive New Orleans accent, a verse from one of his songs:

> I tried to grab that ball and dot the door,
> But he said, you can't play with that ball, boy, you got to sew.
> I said I want to go outside and play with my friends,
> He said you gotta grab those feathers and crimp the ends.
>
> So I grabbed those feathers with a boot on my face,
> I had to crimp those feathers so I wouldn't be late.
> And at that point in my life I had to make a decision,
> But I knew in my heart I had to listen.

Romeo is not shy in admitting his reluctance to commit to the tradition as a child: "I didn't love that shit. At ten years old you don't care about that." But now he's at a point in his life where he has accepted and made peace with his past as he's become a husband and father in his own right: "I'm glad I went through all that shit because it made me realize I'm not going to choose this shit over them [his family], you know what I mean? Even though this is my life. I swear to God I love this shit."

Romeo is ebullient about his love for the culture, the tradition, his tribe, and especially the craftsmanship he displays year after year: "When people say every year you make a new suit, this is the thing about me, the reason I sew the way I sew, is because some people might sew, in 2007 you might wear a lime-green suit with a blue sky and the green grass. [In] 2008 you might wear an orange suit with a blue sky and the green grass. I don't do that." Romeo suggested other Indians may play it safe in their sewing so that if they get behind they "can pick something from the last suit" and the audience of onlookers wouldn't be able to know. Romeo is emphatic that he doesn't take the safe route in his sewing, and he uses his total recall of his past creations to prove his point. "In 2007 I wore blue sky and green grass," he began. "In 2008, I wore orange sky with the desert sand. 2009 I wore yellow sky with water. 2010 I wore snow scenery. 2011 I wore . . . You know what I'm saying? If I was to take something from the snow suit and put the sand on there, that bitch would stick out like a sore thumb because it's two totally different sceneries. That's why you can't. I never wore the same thing."

Every Indian has a different reason for creating a new suit every year. Whereas Romeo's reason is to make sure he stands out and garners the hard-fought respect of other Chiefs and tribes, Tootie Montana's stated reason for making a new suit every year was so that other Indians couldn't figure out the construction methods he used in creating his suits. Mimicking others, he said, "People say, 'Why y'all make a new suit every year?'" "Well, we better," he said, answering the would-be detractors, "because if you don't, if I kept this suit, and this would be my suit every year, by the time the guys see me so many times they'd know, figure how this go, and we all gonna be looking alike one time. So when they see this, that's the idea behind it, that's the thing where the thrill come in. When they see you this year, next year you come out different. Every year different, every year different, and you throw 'em off. They can't copy."

Tootie famously sewed his suits with his wife, Joyce. Similarly, Romeo Bougere sews with his wife. "I've never dated a woman that didn't sew. If you don't sew I don't mess with you . . . This is sacred to me," he said with his hand over his sewing table covered in a half-beaded patch. "I love it and I want to keep it that way . . . So, if you come into my world and you sew, it's like okay, you gon' give me 25 and I'm gon' give you 25 percent because you gon' do this, which is gon' make me like you, and then I'm a start wanting to do things with you."

Sewing as part of a family activity is the same for cousins Keelian Boyd and Charles Duvernay of the Young Maasai Hunters. Both sew with their wives. Boyd, who is the Big Chief of the tribe said, "I get more enjoyment out of watching cuz," he said pointing to Charles's wife, Jennie Wimbish, who sews suits but doesn't mask herself. Boyd described her as "a master sewer" before detailing his joy at seeing his own wife, Shawmika Edwards Boyd, pulling up a chair to sew beside him. He said: "You always hear about the Indians, but it's the hearts of those folks who put us . . . make us . . . make sure that we hit the street. You know you don't hear enough about them . . . Like Tootie had Ms. Joyce, but if he didn't tell you about Ms. Joyce, you wouldn't know about Ms. Joyce. Everybody have a Ms. Joyce. You need them. You need them."

Whether it's a Ms. Joyce, a Jennie Wimbish, or Shawmika Boyd, putting together one Indian suit takes a village, a fact Gilbert "Cosmo" Dave knows a lot about. Dave has never masked Indian. Though his mother promised he could mask when he turned eighteen, he's never put on a suit, because she died when he was seventeen. "She passed away, so I just like . . . I ain't wanna mask," he said. "I wanted to continue to sew and the suits I made for the people who allowed me to do it my way; I basically was making my suits, you know, but they wore it."

In the summer of 2020, when he was sixty-four years old, Cosmo's grief at losing his mother so young—and before she could see him take part in a tradition and a culture he loved and participated in from an early age—was still apparent. Cosmo's mother was a seamstress. "I used to watch her make gowns and stuff, and it was fascinating," Cosmo said reminiscing on his time as a child. "She let me play with it. I'd be running through the house, and she would stop me in dead run, [saying] 'Come here! Thread that needle.' And I would grab it, my eyes were young then. And then like on rainy days, I'd get bored of coloring and writing in a book [and say], 'Hey mama, can I get some thread and needle.' [She'd say,] 'Yeah,' [and] I'd sit there and she give

Gilbert “Cosmo” Dave, with a suit he is working on. Photograph by author.

me some little trinket and I'd go in my room and I'd start sewing it down, because that's what I like, I just wanted to do it."

Cosmo's love for sewing grew after he saw his brother-in-law mask with the 9th Ward Flaming Arrows back in the 1960s. "That was the oldest, biggest gang they had in the Ninth Ward," Cosmo said. "The gang was so big they had three of everything: three Spies, three Flags, three Queens, you know, three Big Chiefs . . . It just was something you had to grow up and see. It was great, beautiful." Although Cosmo's longing to mask remained unfulfilled in his youth, he continued to sew, much to his mother's delight. He remembered hearing her brag to her customers, "Look at what my son made."

Now, in her absence, he has continued to sew, longing to one day don one of his own creations but not feeling right about doing so without her. He said his friends tell him often: "You know that's what your mama wanted you to do. You need to do it so you can release a lot of whatever is in your heart." In recounting the encouragement of his friends, Cosmo was wistful in his answer, "I keep saying one day, one day, but I ain't did it yet, though?"

Still, Cosmo's contribution to the culture is undeniable. The late Ronald W. Lewis, who founded the Choctaw Hunters tribe in the Lower Ninth Ward as well as the House of Dance and Feathers museum on the property behind his home on Tupelo Street, said Cosmo was "one of the greatest Indian sewers who never wore a suit."

In hearing the accolade, Cosmo was demure then, as he was when we talked more than ten years after his story was first recorded for the Neighborhood Story Project: "I enjoy creating the suits. There are people in the shadows that make Mardi Gras happen. That's how

I look at myself. I love to go out on Carnival day to see how people react to the suit—I love being behind it and representing it. Let's go get 'em! I got a needle and thread stuffed in my back pocket just in case something happen out there on the street. I'm prepared."

A lot goes into the artistry of making an Indian suit, but the act of sewing a complete suit goes beyond just being pretty. There is also a spirituality, rhythm, camaraderie, and a story associated with creating every suit.

Standing in Bo Dollis Jr.'s living room, his sewing table behind me, his 2020 suit in front of me, and with him sitting in the midst of it all, I couldn't help but ask about what he had created. He said, "the whole story goes down." In one patch, an Indian is teaching another Indian "how to shoot a bow and arrow, how to fight." On the two wing patches, a fight scene is depicted; on another patch, the chiefs are coming together with a plan to put an end to the violence. The entire suit is a painstakingly illustrated history of the origins of Black masking Indians from Indigenous tribes that includes scenes of hunting, peace, and concerns over trust. Bo said, "That night before Mardi Gras, we had to get dressed at 8:00 [a.m.]; I was still sewing at 3:00 [a.m.]."

Romeo Bougere became animated as he began talking about the patch he was working on for a new suit (though Mardi Gras for 2021 would later be canceled): "I'm about to put on a suit that I know nobody gon' have . . . I know that I'm gon' stand out because this story is about me. That's me in the middle of that fucking apron. See everybody sewing cowboys and Indians, and the Indians killing the white people and man that story is about me." The canvas patch on his worktable filled with colorful beads depicted Romeo singing in

Indian practice, his father teaching him how to sew. He even went into the slightest of details including the tattoos on his neck, the chains on the spectators' necks, and the details of the kind of cup used for serving in a barroom. Gesticulating toward the different scenes in the suit, he said: "The tambourine look exactly like the tambourine you buy at the store. The boy had a jersey on. The boy Heineken bottle look just like a Heineken bottle."

Suit creations differ for each member of every tribe, especially those wearing beaded flat patches. As Romeo said, some depict Indian scenes, or scenes from the early American West between cowboys and Indians, while others incorporate more African or spiritual elements. Ronnel Butler, who serves as the Gang Flag for 9th Ward Black Hatchet, depicted Jesus falling while carrying the cross on the chest patch of his 2020 suit. On the apron there were more Christian scenes, including Samson breaking his chains and collapsing the columns of the Philistine temple of Dagon, as well as a scene of Moses leading the Israelites out of Egypt and through the Red Sea.

Cherice Harrison Nelson, daughter of Donald Harrison Sr., has embraced, like her father, the African roots of the masking tradition. As the Maroon Queen of the Guardians of the Flame Maroon Society, she said: "I wear African attire. I wear geles, I wear African head wraps all the time, just about 99 percent of the time. People tell me more often than not, 'I love your costume.' That is not my costume. Those are my clothes." When it comes to her participating in the masking tradition, Cherice said she feels more like she is unmasked no matter how elaborate or simple her suit for the year may be. "You can't tell me I need to cover myself in beads," she said. "That's what you may

Cherice Harrison Nelson, 2019. Courtesy Henry York.

want to do for yourself, [but] if I put three beads on my suit, and I'm okay with it, and I walk out the door, and it tells a story because I am a narrative artist, and if my suit tells a story that I am telling, then it is okay with me." In this unmasking and paying homage to the African roots of the tradition, Cherice said she is "the sum total of everything that went before," including her ancestors and ancestral homeland.

Her position on the roots of the culture and how it is depicted is aligned very much to her father's. She noted that when he returned to the masking tradition in the late 1980s after taking twenty years off to raise his family, the first suit he made as the Big Chief of the Guardians of the Flame had "an Oba for Benin on it": "My father definitely believed that this was African cultural expression refashioned

ME TOO

for where we are geographically and cloaked, and that is the mask. The cloaking of the African ways of being and expression."

All the work that goes into a suit, the repetitive sewing that can send participants into a trance, the storytelling from patch to patch and design to design, along with various influences behind those patches and designs, be they African, Indigenous, or from tribe members' own lives, all comes down to the debut of the suit on Mardi Gras morning—a feeling the participants say is like no other.

"I'm a totally different person when it comes down to Mardi Gras," Bo Dollis Jr. said when I asked what it felt like to finally wear one of his creations he worked on for a year or more: "Once I put on a suit you will not catch me smiling. I have friends right now that I have been friends with since high school that won't come see me." Romeo Bougere expressed the same sentiment about how he feels when he gets dressed Mardi Gras morning: "When you put that joint on in here and you walk out that door, you go from being Romeo, to uh . . . I don't know what I'm called in the fucking spiritual world." And just like Bo, Romeo has friends and family members who refuse to see him on Mardi Gras day because of the sudden change in his personality: "My cousins and them, they'll tell you, I have cousins that be like, 'Man listen, I don't fuck with him when he in his Indian suit.' They tell me that because I'm a different person."

Donald Harrison Sr.'s sister-in-law, Efzelda Coleman, described the spirit taking over her son in the family-produced documentary *Guardians of the Flame: New Orleans Mardi Gras Indians:* "If you ever

Opposite: Cherice Harrison Nelson masked for carnival. Courtesy Arthur Severio.

had the opportunity to be in a spiritual church and see how the spirit will jump from one person to the other, you will definitely understand." She said her son went into a "utopia" when he masked as the Wild Man with the Guardians of the Flame. "It was just like being in a religious service and you hear people say they feel the spirit," Coleman said before offering some final words of wisdom on the spiritual element of the culture: "I would say to any child who has the experience to mask Mardi Gras Indian, I think they would come into a real revelation of what it is for soul and spirit to meet. You have to take it out of the natural. It's a spiritual experience, and when you look at people masking, you can see the transition that comes in them."

"It's just something that come over you," Joe Jenkins, the late Chief who died in 2020, said in the *Guardians of the Flame* documentary.

On Mardi Gras morning that "something" comes over you, but it is something the Black masking Indians have been working toward all year long. In addition to the painstaking labor of sewing on their suits daily, they've also attended Indian practice weekly if not more. During these practices the Indians in attendance dance and sing songs. Some of the songs are new and composed and rehearsed by the Indians of that specific gang, such as those brought into popularity by Bo Dollis Sr. and his funk group named after his tribe, the Wild Magnolias.

"Handa Wanda is something he made," Bo Dollis Jr. said about his father's musical legacy within the Black masking Indian tradition. "Handa Wanda doesn't have a meaning. He had a Honda car, and the next-door neighbor was named Wanda, so when he got to the studio they just made Handa Wanda, and it just became one of the greatest hits for New Orleans Mardi Gras."

Other songs are more traditional such as "Shallow Water" "Fiyah Water," "Iko Iko," "Two Way Pockey Way," and the sacred hymn "Indian Red." These songs have meanings. Dollis Jr. said: "Hey Pockey Way, means you go this way, I'm a go that way. Jock a Mo Fi Na Nay means kiss my ass . . . Shallow Water is like a slave song. What it was is they was singing to each other, letting us know like what we about to do. Like, 'Okay y'all we got some shallow water coming keep singing and we gon' cross over it before the masters get here.'"

In these traditional songs, especially in the aforementioned "Shallow Water" and "Iko Iko," Indians can practice "throwing slang" or doing an improvisational freestyle of their own lyrics similar to the freestyle battles that happen between dueling rappers in hip-hop. By practicing their freestyles among their own tribe during Indian practice, each member has a chance to tighten up their lyrics in an attempt to best another tribe or gang when they meet on Mardi Gras morning.

These songs, accompanied by tambourine playing and dancing, are rehearsed during Indian practice, which generally takes place on Sunday evening, keeping the tradition of the singing, dancing, and drumming of Congo Square alive. In addition to Indian practice there is also signal practice. As noted in chapter 1, when Black masking Indians emerge and parade the streets, they use secretive hand signals that allow them to communicate without speaking. These gestures are learned during signal practice so that the members of a tribe can communicate among themselves in a secret nonverbal code when they're parading or meeting another tribe.

These codified practices, a year's worth of work sewing and practicing, culminate in that "something" that comes over Black masking

Indians who get dressed on Mardi Gras morning. They walk out of their doors to the waiting crowds who make up the second line in confidence and full possession of the spirit of their ancestors, their God, and pride in their work. They walk across the city, uptown and downtown, meeting other tribes, ribbing one another even more than in the trash talk traded throughout the year. "It's a warrior culture so as I'm sitting down sewing . . . we sit down and we talk shit to each other every time we see each other," Romeo Bougere said of the barbs that go back and forth ahead of Mardi Gras Day. One of the exclamations he's fond of is, "I'm a bust your ass," meaning beating a rival in prettiness while wearing an Indian suit. But even in all of his posturing and that of other Indians from the old legends like Tootie Montana and Donald Harrison Sr. to the young legends in the making, the title of who's the prettiest, who did the best work, who killed their rival dead with needle and thread, and who has the most dominant tribe can't honestly and objectively be determined unless it's by two men or women meeting as rivals, but equals.

Donald Harrison Sr. acknowledged he met his match one day, telling biographer Al Kennedy, "I swear he was pretty." But what he couldn't make up for in the beauty of his suit, Harrison said, he made up for in his singing and dancing performance of playing Indian. In this way, well before Romeo Bougere was born, Harrison illustrated what Bougere would later say was the most honest thing you could ever hear from an Indian: "In your heart as a Mardi Gras Indian you know who won and who lost. In your heart, when you stand in front that man, and you see him on the other end of the tube, man you know who won and who lost."

A NEW GENERATION

There is a through line in modern Mardi Gras Indian culture, and that is the evolution that continues from one generation to another. Along with the evolution there is innovation as each son or daughter etches out their own lane to establish their unique identity. Just as Tootie Montana innovated decades after his great-uncle Becate, the same goes for the generation of Cherice Harrison Nelson and Donald Harrison Jr., who innovated and evolved the culture after learning from their father, and the same can be said of Romeo Bougere and Bo Dollis Jr., who continue to move the culture forward as they bring the children in their lives—their own, cousins, family members, or kids in the community—along for the ride.

"Everything about Indian," is how Romeo Bougere responded when asked what he learned from his father, the late Big Chief Rudy Bougere: "I learned how to sew. I learned how to basically build suits, basically play Indian, which is . . . the main things like signals." But in this culture this learning does not happen in a vacuum. Even as the son or daughter of a Big Chief this education comes from not only your parent who's partaking in the tradition but your entire tribe and the culture at large. Bougere said: "I can say I learned how to sew from him but it's like I learned how to sew also from other people . . . I learned how to sew a different way, different techniques . . . because you gotta keep in mind, he died when I was like seventeen, so it's not, I didn't get a chance to really do the adult side of this with him."

Even in that lack of sharing an experience as an adult rather than a boy, Bougere recalled one moment that stands out in his mind when he made his transition from just the son of a Big Chief to a Black masking Indian in his own right. "I didn't really get an opportunity to really mingle with the adults and all that under his wing, until I jumped off the porch in 2001 when I masked Gang Flag," Bougere said. "That was my first time ever building my own whole suit, right, and then you know, and that's when I started meeting the big boys."

Bo Dollis Jr.'s introduction to the culture was through his father. He said their story parallels because his father also got in trouble for first trying to mask Indian at the age of thirteen in the late 1950s: "He made his Indian suit by his next-door neighbor house. On Mardi Gras morning, he stayed on Jackson Avenue where the Zulu passed. He ran out the house, and my grandparents thought, 'Oh he just going to Zulu,' not knowing he's going to put on a whole Indian suit. So he snuck and made that, coming from Second and Dryades he—turned on Oretha Castle Haley now—turned on Jackson, [and] my grandfather was standing on the corner and that's when he got busted." But this initiation into the Mardi Gras Indians for Bo Dollis Sr. at just thirteen led to him becoming Big Chief at the age of fifteen just two years later. "His Chief wound up getting drunk or something like that and the gang told him, 'Now you gotta think about it,'" Bo recounted.

This story aligns with how a chief is installed, because while masking Indian is traditionally a family affair, it may not always be so. "Most times it's a lot of passing down," Bo said. "Now if I [didn't] have a child that masked Indian, I'll pick somebody in my group and be like, 'Well you can sew Indian suits, you can sing, you can dance, so now I'm a train you to be a chief so when I do step down you can take it over.' You can just take like a normal person and train them to be a chief."

Keelian Boyd remembers growing up with Indian culture all around him before he started masking at the age of twelve in the tribe of his cousin Big Chief Tyrone Stevenson, the Monogram Hunters in the Seventh Ward: "We always had family members that was Indians. Uncles, cousins, neighbors, that was always affiliated with it. My grandmother sewed a bunch of Indian costumes . . . so it was kind of like I was born into it, you know, and one thing led to another."

Boyd, who now serves as the Big Chief of the Young Maasai Hunters, masks with his cousin Charles Duvernay, who is the Flag Boy in the tribe. Duvernay says while he always wanted to mask as a child, he's happy he finally got into the tradition as an adult. "One cousin in particular through marriage, Spy Boy Wingy [Franklin Davis with the Yellow Pocahontas], he really like lit it up for me," Duvernay said. "But my mom wasn't having it at that time, and then getting older, moving away, coming back home, just life you know. You can say I'm a late bloomer, but better late than never." And perhaps because of that late blooming, Duvernay has brought his three daughters, with his wife, Jennie Wimbish, into the tradition. In a side room off of the living room in their New Orleans East home stood five Indian suits—two for adults and three for children. They were Duvernay's 2019 and 2020 suits, and the 2020 suits for his daughters, full in feathers and beaded patches from crown to matching moccasin boots.

One of Duvernay's daughters, Sadie, who was eight years old at the time, said she liked masking "because it's fun" and "sometimes" helped out with the sewing of the costumes. Duvernay's bringing his daughters into the tradition so early is similar to other chiefs and their families who have immersed their children into the culture.

Cherice Harrison Nelson recalls that while her father, Donald Harrison Sr., started Guardians of the Flame after taking a twenty-year break to raise his family, when he returned to the culture he loved, it was with his children and grandchildren: "He said: 'Participating in the tradition is not a halfway house. Either you're in or you're out, and if you're in you have to be willing to give two things; your time and your money,'" Cherice recalled. "Once we were all adults he decided to come back and not only to . . . to bring an elevated awareness to some of his friends who were older like him and no longer masked, [but] to also give insight to a bygone era of the tradition; especially with the suiting and the singing styles."

In the 1993 *Guardians of the Flame* documentary, it is noted that the new tribe Donald Harrison Sr. brought out in 1989 featured three generations of Harrison men. Of the name, Guardians of the Flame, he said he chose it to "express the desire that I guard the tradition. The tradition is the flame, [and to] pass it down to younger generations and let them know they will one day be a Guardian of the Flame and pass it down to generations after them."

In the documentary a young Brian Harrison Nelson, who was then a Little Chief in the tribe, said, "If a little child has never seen a Mardi Gras Indian, I could be the first one they ever saw, and they can go and pass the tradition down." As an adult, and now Big Chief of the Guardians of the Flame, Brian has continued the work of his family to educate people about the culture of Black masking Indians. He directed the theatrical film *Keeper of the Flame* as his thesis when

On the following four pages: Indian suits on display inside the Duvernay home. Photographs by author.

he earned an MFA in cinematic arts from the University of Southern California in 2011 and is currently filming a documentary entitled *Hail to the Queens,* exploring the Black masking Indian tradition from a woman's perspective.

This passing of the tradition, be it through family and community or through film, music, and books, is what keeps the tradition going in each successive generation. With African, Indigenous, European, and religious roots that syncretized after centuries of contact—first on the African continent and then in the New World—the tradition of Black masking Indians is one that moves like the mighty, muddy river that helps define and identify the city where these tribes were founded and where they carry out their ancient traditions in communal expression.

In or out of an Indian suit, these men and women, girls and boys, are immersed in a culturally specific tradition that subsumes their entire selves in the name of something greater. For those who participate in the tradition, adult or child, it is more than a mask and more than a costume for Carnival. It is an ancestral reconnection encoded into their DNA. As Donald Harrison Sr. told biographer Al Kennedy, "I was born to mask with the Indians." As were his children, grandchildren, and the various men, women, and children whose voices vibrate through this very text. Being born to mask Indian, or even incited and inspired to mask Indian by the passing of the gangs on Carnival day, St. Joseph's Night, or Super Sunday, or seeing them perform live at Jazz Fest—larger than life—sets in the soul a new way of life, a new way of thinking and perceiving, and a new way of being. Participating in this cultural tradition provides a filter through which to see and be in the world, and adds a unique perspective on issues social, cultural, and even economic. Beyond the beauty they bear when they are suited and booted in a headdress of feathers and beads and armed with a staff or flag, it is the bravado of their attitudes, the delicate intricacy with which they create, and the excitement and magic in how they discuss what they do that exudes a magical, alchemistic truth that is undeniably apparent in their actions, reactions, and interactions in everyday life. Simply put, they live Indian.

3
Living Indian

"To live Indian is, it's just like waking up every day," Stafford Agee said during our impromptu interview in the basement of my aunt's Seventh Ward home just off A. P. Tureaud in New Orleans. "Some people wake up, they go to work, and they have a job to do. There's people, they wake up, and they're thinking about Indian. They go to sleep, they're thinking about Indian. Everything that they do, it includes Indian."

Agee's explanation of what it means to live as a Black masking Indian 24/7/365 depicts a lifestyle and culture that is indeed all its own for the men, women, and children who participate in it whether they're in their suits or not. What is most noticeable is that while the figure or symbol of Black masking Indians looms larger than life and is elevated to that of A-list celebrity status in the city, the participants themselves are everyday men and women who lead normal, quotidian lives. Those who mask also have jobs, responsibilities, families, and communities that they serve, and living Indian informs how they show up in each capacity.

AT WORK

Stafford Agee is a musician. He plays the trombone for Rebirth Brass Band, with credits on seventeen albums and guest appearances on fifteen other albums. "I've been a musician for thirty-seven years," he said. "[I'm a] mentor. Good friend. I'm just a part of the community."

Romeo Bougere is also a musician as part of the Mardi Gras Indian hip-hop duo 79rs Gang; his day job is working with the New Orleans Recreational Development Commission (NORD). Bo Dollis Jr. and Ronnel Butler both work as barbers. Bo is also a musician playing with the funk band of his tribe, the Wild Magnolias. Keelian Boyd has worked as a crane operator at the Domino sugar refinery for more than ten years, and his cousin Charles Duvernay recently secured a position at Domino to test sugar products after working as a sales manager for another company. Cherice Harrison Nelson is an educator. In all of these different jobs and occupations, Indian is always there; the culture is always calling, demanding of its denizens their time, attention, love, care, craftsmanship, work ethic—mind, body, and soul.

For Romeo and Bo, they are Big Chief everywhere they go. "I'm one of those guys Indian at my job too, they call me Big Chief at work," Bougere said. "Where you at, Big Chief?," he hollered, mimicking the way his coworkers call for him. "All day that's all I hear, 'What's up, Big Chief?,' so it's like even if I try to leave that shit alone, it just follows me."

Bo Dollis Jr. embraces the hail of "Big Chief" following him throughout his day. In his living room, our interview was pointed and uninterrupted, conditions he said would not have been present if we had conducted the conversation outside of his salon. "If we had did the interview outside my shop, y'all would of got aggravated because so many people start to blowing," he said. The attention has even changed his habits. "I stopped even standing outside of my shop because they just be blowing for no reason. Like, 'Alright Chief.' I'm like, 'Hey, how y'all doing,' you know."

Cousins Keelian and Charles say they try to distance themselves from the culture, but it doesn't always work. "Sometimes we still deal with Mardi Gras because we have a what we call NOMGI Sip and Sew—it's the New Orleans Mardi Gras Indian Sip and Sew Experience," Boyd said. Then he added: "We try not to do Mardi Gras every day. You know, we try to just live and just have fun and just talk about it when we get close."

But even when those who mask are not actively thinking about Indian, Indian is actively calling them, like a restless ancestor in the spirit realm, demanding to be acknowledged. In this way Cherice Harrison Nelson has created a communal and evolutionary experience in her growth in the culture thanks to her career as an educator.

"I'm a lifelong student," Harrison Nelson began after I asked how her background in education influenced the trajectory of her work in the culture today. Through traditional avenues of study as well as informal, independent study and indulging her curiosity on her own, she acknowledged that everything she does as an artist evolves: "Especially [as] an artist within an Indigenous cultural tradition the challenge for me is what do I keep? What stays standard and traditional and what evolves? The evolution can occur in a number of ways. It can be in the ways the suit is constructed, it can be the color choice, it can

be the content, it can be the story I'm telling, it can be the style of the suit, it can be the style of the headdress, the use of materials. Where are the evolutions, and what's the thing that remains constant? For me the constant is narrative beadwork. Aurora Borealis rhinestones, plumes, and, you know, hopefully some ribbons or something else that has some motion so that when I dance there's some motion to the suit, some fluidity."

How Harrison Nelson's life study influences what she creates year after year in the Black masking tradition is similar to how Tootie Montana expressed how his background in construction as a lather helped influence how he constructed his suits. Once participants are embedded in the culture of Indian, a constant transference of ideas and inspiration occurs and influences them as they sew a new suit every year. Masking Indian is a pursuit that can ruin finances, marriages, childhoods, and even bodily function, in the name of feeding the insatiable appetite of the culture that demands more, bigger, better, greater, and prettier from its peoples year after year.

IN RELATIONSHIPS

"When he first started masking, he didn't have such elaborate suits like he does now," Joyce Montana began, in the documentary *Tootie's Last Suit*. "Tootie and I both had full-time jobs at the time, so when I'd come home in the evenings, I would start cooking, have my sewing on the table, and I'd be sewing and cooking, sewing and cooking." Of his wife's dedication to a craft and a culture she married into, Montana

Opposite: Cherice Harrison Nelson. Courtesy Arthur Severio.

said: "My wife, Joyce, she something. Without her I couldn't have done it. I couldn't have done it. And I put her against anybody who work on Indian suits sewing. I don't care what it is. They don't come nowhere near her."

Interspersed in this story of Tootie's adoration of his wife and her description of essentially working a second job is footage of the couple sewing together at their dining room table. Feathers and beads abound on the surface of the table you can't even see, along with a white sewing machine whose hum is distinguishable against the silent backdrop of beads that tinkle against a needle every now and again. By the looks of things, theirs was a marriage made strong in the culture. But that is not everyone's story.

"You can't be an Indian every day," Fred Johnson, former Spy Boy for the Yellow Pocahontas, said in the documentary. "You're an Indian one, or two, or three days out of a year, in costume. A lot of guys who masked Indian didn't keep a job. A lot of guys who masked Indian was in and out of jail, part-time or sometime drug users." His assertion matches what Robbe Lee told biographer Al Kennedy, that to be an Indian was to be "rough." And though that may have held true during the violent era of Indian culture in the early to mid-twentieth century, what seems to exist now is a more family-friendly, community-oriented endeavor, if only those at the top of a tribe's pecking order choose to maintain such a disciplined ideal.

"Mardi Gras Indian to me is everything," Romeo Bougere said. "It's just a way of life for me because it has picked me up, broke me down, ruined my life, bettered my life, it messed up my marriage, and then me and my wife got back together. Everything, it's like a life for me."

Bougere said he had to learn to find balance in his responsibilities as a husband and father and Big Chief of the 9th Ward Hunters. He readily acknowledges that sewing is his full-time second job: "It picks me up because it eliminates and erases any negative thought that I have, so I have to be focused." But that singular focus can cause a rift in family dynamics, leaving spouses and children feeling neglected and ignored, another fact Bougere readily admits: "You tend to neglect the important things." In referring to his wife, he said, "Sometimes she want to go out, I don't want to go out." He was staunch in his admission of his own part in contributing to the shaky dynamics in his relationship. His tunnel vision and myopic view of the world and himself as only a heavy-hitting Big Chief, creating at a level he believes sets the standard for what other Indians should aspire to and compete against, made him arrogant and verbose in his reaction to his family's aversion to his love of all things Indian. A reaction similar to the one he had as a child when he wanted to play football with friends but was forbidden to because of his sewing responsibilities. His lack of empathy at the cycle he's continuing is telling as he references his wife's and children's interactions and how he responds with: "You mad, you pissed off? You'll be alright." If his children were to ask him to go somewhere, his answer is normally a curt, "Not today." But in telling this story, he also recognized his flaws. "I couldn't be like that."

In his effort to adjust his priorities and spend more time with his wife and children, Bougere said they began to notice a change in him: "They sense like okay, 'Well he not in his element so he not happy like he should be, he's a little cranky.' Then I get this. I get the wife waking up sometimes saying, 'Man, you need to go fuckin' sew, man!'"

His struggle to balance his priorities as a husband and father were palpable as it was happening in real time. The demands he faced from his young cousin sitting across from him at his sewing table, waiting for him to finish his interview so they could get back to beading the patch they were working on, was a constant reminder during the conversation that while his mind may always be on Indian, even in discussing it, his heart would always be in the work of his latest creation for his next suit.

The Indian life subsumes his entire being, from the way he's addressed at work, to the traditional Indian songs he sings to himself to get through the day, to the second job he takes on when he comes home and sits at his worktable. The culture is always present, closer than a shadow, more than a spirit; rather, it is a living, breathing being, exacting and demanding that he give to the culture he's been immersed in since childhood.

Donald Harrison Sr. knew he could not commit to living Indian as well as to being a present husband and father. He hung up his suit for twenty years after masking from 1949 to 1968. He told a *Meschabe* interviewer: "The reason I didn't mask for so many years was, I was raising a family. I want to mask, but I didn't have the energy. No, energy is not the right word. The get-up-and-go, the drive, to really get down and sew." However, when he returned to the culture he loved since he was a small child, he did it with his family in tow. His wife, Herreast, and daughters, Michele, Cara, and Cherice, all took part in the beading for the suits that the Guardians of the Flame would wear when they debuted in 1989. "He did not like to have anyone outside of a family member sewing for him," Herreast Harrison told biographer Al Kennedy.

In making Indian culture a family affair, Big Chiefs, Big Queens, Flag Boys, Spy Boys, and anyone holding a position in a tribe can bring those they love into the culture they love just as much. But the culture is ravenous. Just as easily as it can bring a family together to sew, to sing, and to practice in the barroom on a Sunday night, it can just as easily tear a family apart, and not only due to a difference in lifestyle choices as what happened with Romeo Bougere and his wife. Just as financial problems are one of the leading causes of divorce, so, too, can they be a leading cause of a Black masking Indian divorcing the culture he or she loves, which doesn't always love them back.

MAKING ENDS MEET

"I never said anything more to him than it was expensive, and 'I don't know if we can afford it,'" Herreast Harrison told biographer Al Kennedy regarding the conversations she had with her husband, Donald Harrison Sr., before he decided to hang up his suit to focus on his family.

"If I sit down to add up every little thing, I know, I'd quit," Bo Dollis Jr. said when asked how much it costs to make one suit.

"One pound of these feathers, which is only like seventy-five [feathers] is like $450, and these stones are like $10 each, and the beads you get . . . Oh man, it's costly, it's expensive," Ronnel Butler said. "I have a suit right now and it's . . . it cost me like eight, nine thousand dollars to make. Easy."

Keelian Boyd. Courtesy Matthew Hinton.

“I don’t think there’s nothing in the world—and I’m going to be honest with you—that you can stress out more than Indian,” Romeo Bougere said. “If you taking it as serious as we do, you realize that you won’t pay a bill to mask.”

“I don’t care how much it costs,” Keelian Boyd said defiantly. “We find ways to make money, but, if I didn’t make that money, I still would make that suit.”

The tradition of making a new Indian suit every year comes with a well-acknowledged financial strain, and that was true long before the massive creations Black masking Indians come up with now. In 1928 the editorial writers of the *Louisiana Weekly* mocked Indian gangs that, they said, "strutted about the city like a peacock, looking at our fine feathers, forgetting our home ties and our obligations to our grocer, baker and candlestick maker." The editors went on to say that those who masked knew "that no bill collectors will be dunning us for those installments that we let pass so that we could mask for Carnival."

The late Big Chief Robbe Lee, who first masked in 1929—one year after the mocking *Louisiana Weekly* article—told biographer Al Kennedy that he found a way to make an Indian suit without going into debt. He invested his time and money in the tradition for thirty years—some of that time when the nation was in the grips of the Great Depression. He recalled how some men could only pay to have a suit made for them because they had money, while others who were short of cash would sell or pawn their suits. Of those men, Robbe said, they'd "make a suit, then get broke, and go to Dryades Street and pawn it or sell it."

Bo Dollis Jr., who learned from his father, said it was cheaper during his dad's time to make a suit: "They were getting stuff out of their wives' closet, old jewelry, and things like that to make the Indian suits, and you know, New Orleans had a bunch of chickens running around so that's where the feathers was coming from." Actually, it was turkey feathers the old-school Indians used to wear, gathered from the abundance of wild turkeys in the city, but even in these meager times, Black masking Indians found a way to be pretty. But like fashion, the culture changed with the times, and expenses began to creep up even more.

"They started wearing velvet [and it] got a little bit more expensive," Bo said. "They start making stuff look bigger, and like right now it's real expensive 'cause things are getting way out of hand." What does out of hand look like? How does it add up? Bo ran the numbers:

> Feathers right now, you're looking at $300 a pound, okay. We might use up to five or six pounds on an average Chief suit . . . Then you talk about velvet. Velvet is $20 a yard. So on an average you might use between ten to fifteen yards, okay. And that's not counting the beads. Beads is about the cheapest thing on the whole Indian suit. Then you not counting the decoration, whatever you want, the little accents, or the ribbon, the fluff, the tips. So, yeah, I think if I would sit down and have to save every receipt, yeah, I'd quit. I'd be done. I'll retire. I'll throw in the hat like, "That's it y'all, I'm down," but it's a pretty penny.

Yet, even in knowing the cost per yard and per pound and the sacrifice it takes to purchase materials, it is only half-heartedly that Dollis says he'd quit the culture if he knew the full dollar amount spent to make the suits for himself and his seventeen tribe members. Even this acknowledgment of costliness fuels his creativity. As he discussed his work on his next suit, he said it was all about sacrifices. "As Mardi Gras Indians we have to do so much sacrificing," Bo said. "[There's] time without family, what money we gon' use. You know we gotta take a little bit from this bill and go put it on this Indian suit, you know take a little from that bill . . . and just as masking Indian we have to do a whole lot of sacrificing."

Ronnel Butler was reticent to acknowledge the sacrifices made in the name of masking. "Can't say that on television," he said into the camera recording the interview. But with some coaxing he readily admitted that "some guys sacrifice marriage because it don't coincide with you sewing . . . You want to go hang with your friends, but you can't because you gotta mask, and if [you] go hang out with them for ten hours then [you lose] out on ten hours of sewing. It's a lot of sacrificing, money-wise. MONEY."

When he got to the word "money," he dragged out the two syllables, incredulous at the amount of money he was spending to fuel what most would consider a hobby for the privileged. But it is not the privileged who mask Indian; it is the proven, the anointed and appointed. Those who don't let dollar amounts, nagging friends, wives, and/or children stop them from participating in a tradition that makes them feel free, energized, loved, adored, and connected to something bigger than themselves.

"You buy what you need, but then you buy stuff you just see," Keelian Boyd said about how making an Indian suit can get out of hand. Imitating his reaction when shopping for materials, he said: "You know like, 'Oh, man look at them stones!' You may not even use them for that suit, but you're just like, 'Aaah, I'm a grab 'em,' and then, you know, you ain't grabbing five; you grabbing 200."

In sourcing the materials, the Indians order from everywhere. Although they patronize local businesses as much as possible in the New Orleans area, they're also ordering materials from New York,

Los Angeles, and as far away as China. That's another factor that can stress an already stressed-out Indian. "When you waiting Mardi Gras Day and your feathers is not here, man, you trying to figure out a way to go steal them things out the store," Romeo Bougere said. "I'm just being honest. I'm just telling you the truth. By any means."

Perhaps this is why a Mardi Gras Indian suit is never really complete. It's the compounding of factors of sewing by hand, sewing after work, buying materials when there is money to do so, and the elaborate nature of the costumes and designs that keep them from being finished. "Some people they just can never get finished with an idea, and it takes them two years to sew," Stafford Agee said.

At the time of this writing, Mardi Gras Indians had to wait another year before they could truly put on and parade in an Indian suit, due to the lasting effects of the COVID-19 global pandemic—caused by the novel coronavirus (discussed in depth in the next chapter)—as New Orleans mayor LaToya Cantrell announced Mardi Gras would be canceled for 2021 in late 2020. When I interviewed the subjects, who speak throughout this text, about the possibility of Mardi Gras being canceled, they all acknowledged it could happen, and yet they were all still sewing, investing their time, and spending their money on materials they were later banned from putting on to parade. (Some did still dress and take pictures for social media to commemorate the 2021 Carnival season.)

"I'll still be sewing," Bo Dollis Jr. said. "I'm a be bigger and bigger. I'm a look like a Mardi Gras float if I keep on sewing like this." In his flippancy was the subtle subtext of, "I don't care." Just as Keelian

Boyd said, "If I didn't make that money, I still would make that suit." Masking Indian is not about money, no matter how plentiful or scarce it may be. Sitting down to sew on canvas or cardboard is not about the time spent away from family, friends, and loved ones, how much your back hurts, or your eyesight is going (Big Chief Robbe Lee's sister blamed her brother's blindness later in life on his sewing). Creating wearable works of art is not even about how much money each Indian could get for them on the open market if they participated in the culture only for profit, as they readily acknowledged some Indians do.

"This flag right here, if I was just to sell this, as it is, right now to anybody in the museum I could get about five thousand dollars for it," Ronnel Butler said of the 9th Ward Black Hatchet gang flag he made for his position for his 2020 suit. Romeo Bougere said the same of the patch he was working on for 2021: "I could sell this patch, man, look at this shit, I could sell this shit for over twenty thousand dollars. Just this one. Completed." Yet he knows he won't, no matter how much the patch is worth, no matter how much a museum curator or private collector would be willing to pay for it, because he knows, even in his ire, that the money is not the point: "People ain't got just like four, five thousand dollars to just throw away. You spending three grand on feathers. People ain't got that kinda money to just throw away, bro." The expense has nothing to do with why Black masking Indians spend every waking moment preparing to mask, living Indian. They do it for the love. The love of the culture, the love of their tribe, as a way to love on themselves, and for the love of their community.

DOWN WITH THE PEOPLE

Sewing all year long may be a solo act for some. Weekly practices provide a revitalization and rejuvenation to a spirit that can become wearied by the menial and repetitive task of beading. But it is when all the elements of what it means to live Indian come together on Mardi Gras Day, St. Joseph's Night, and Super Sunday that the real practice and purpose of toiling all year long is revealed. As Cherice Harrison Nelson said:

> It is your lifeline to create, to get into a space where you do something that is uniquely yours. [That] can be a life force for you . . . Cultural artists especially of Indigenous art forms, to me, they are spiritual first responders. They let people know, you let yourself know, that in this world of uncertainty, that although I may be a mere human, I am a super being because there's something deep within me; a well of something that I can call upon that can support me, and in the act of supporting me to get up every day and do, just to live, to survive . . . the ancillary benefit of that is it will do that for others. It can be unifying.

That unifying factor is why Black masking Indians play such an important role in their community, to their tribe definitely, especially if they are Big Chief. "A lot of people look up to different people for different reasons," Bo Dollis Jr. said, reflecting on what it means to him to be a Big Chief. "I have a stop-the-violence concert that I do every year . . . We give away school supplies. We give away suits to teenagers so they can go do job interviews." He even works to make sure that children and teens in his neighborhood don't succumb to the pressures of gang violence and street life by bringing in families that have lost children to the street, or an actual coffin to scare them straight: "Being a chief, you have a lot of roles; not within Mardi Gras but outside of Mardi Gras. A lot of people don't understand that when it comes down to Indian, Indian is a big thing in everybody neighborhood, and you have a certain person in your neighborhood that's, *that* Chief. I had to learn that I was *that* Chief growing up . . . Being a Chief is some big shoes," he mused.

In those big shoes, Bo has served as counselor, marriage or relationship mediator, first responder, and surrogate father to some of the members in his own tribe. "I had one, he got into an accident, he called me first before he called the police," Bo said. "I'm looking like, 'Did you call the police? Why are you calling me? I can't help you.' [Then he said,] 'Oh, alright, Chief, I'm a call you right back.' Then he called the [police], then he still called me right back."

There's also the celebrity status in the community that comes with masking Indian. "You want to be the beauty," Ronnel Butler said. But even for him it's deeper than that. Butler's brother used to mask Indian before he passed away in 2013, the first year Ronnel masked. He said making his suit that first year after being around the culture for a long time was a way for him "to keep the culture going." "It's amazing. It's beautiful," he said. Everybody in the community knows me as being a barber, but when they see me as a Mardi Gras Indian, it's like, 'Man, you did this all year by yourself? How you cut hair and mask?'"

In the adoration of the community is the adoration of children, which most warms the hearts of the Black masking Indians—children who want to mask Indian like Robbe Lee in the 1920s, or Donald Harrison Sr. in the 1940s. "After I found out he accepted young people in his house, they didn't have to bring me anymore," Robbe told biographer Al Kennedy, of how he first connected with Brother Tillman, the legendary chief of the Creole Wild West. Kennedy notes in the biography for Big Chief Robbe that "Brother Tillman welcomed children, but he was wary of adults. Tillman did not want the older men to learn the secrets he so freely shared with the youngsters."

In the youngsters of the community lies the future of the culture, of those who will live Indian after being bitten by the bug to mask. During the interview for Bo Dollis Jr., which took place on a Wednesday in July 2020, he said, "Friday, I'm a have house full of kids that's not even mine, but they my Indians [so] they mine." He said when the children come to his house, they stay up all night sewing until four in the morning, and then they're back up and at it again by 9:00 a.m. "I be like, 'How long y'all been up?,'" Bo asked, reenacting his conversation with his young Indians. They reply to him: "Oh we slept about two hours . . . Oh, we like it when we come over here by you because we can get in and sew and stuff like that." Bo said he doesn't mind because they're good kids.

In his home, at his shop, and in his life, he, like so many other Black masking Indians before him, set the standard for excellence, for brilliance, for beauty, and what it means to be a member of a

Opposite: Mardi Gras Indian parade. Courtesy Erroll Lebeau.

community, not just an Indian tribe. One man who embedded himself in the community was the late Ronald W. Lewis, who founded the House of Dance and Feathers. He was entrenched in many Black Mardi Gras customs, including as the gatekeeper for the North Side Skull and Bones Gang and one of the founding members of the Choctaw Hunters in the Lower Ninth Ward in which this author's cousin, Brent Taylor, masked as a child. Before starting the Choctaw Hunters, Lewis sewed for Ricky Gettridge in the Yellow Pocahontas. In the book about his life and museum, he said: "I masked a few little times, too, but I wasn't one of those renowned Mardi Gras Indians. I ended up liking to help out on a suit more than masking."

Lewis also formed the Big 9 Social Aid & Pleasure Club with many of the members of the Choctaw Hunters. With such strong ties to his neighborhood due to his involvement in several communal traditions, his death and absence were felt intensely by those who knew him best, especially his longtime friend Gilbert "Cosmo" Dave.

"Mr. Ronald was some important," Dave began, when asked what his oldest, best friend meant to the community. "He was a leader. He made sure the neighborhood stayed right . . . He was just like a heartbeat of the community I would say . . . Everybody come here and talk to him. There was a problem in the hood, he the first one to come out there and try to straighten it out in a right manner. No matter if it's problems with the police or whatever it is. He was there on the spot."

Not only did Ronald keep tradition in the community along with peace; he also made sure that the peacefulness of the traditions he loved, supported, and participated in were passed down to the next generation. Dave said: "They had little fellas who was growing up

. . . they had little problems, you know, they brought him in here, started showing them how to do this Indian stuff [and] they want to be an Indian." Standing in the middle of the backyard garages that comprise the exhibit rooms of the House of Dance and Feathers, Dave remarked how he and Ronald would make suits for children—no matter the cost—who, now all grown up, continue to mask Indian today because they learned from Ronald. "They was little knuckleheads," Dave said. But after talking with Ronald, the young men straightened up. "[He told them,] 'listen to your family, go to school. You don't do that, you can't be in this gang.' The little kids say, 'Alright, alright.' They come here with their report card, they say, 'Look! Look what I'm doing,' and he say, 'We gon' hook you up this year,' and we'd make them an Indian suit, and they'd march with us, and as they got older they started making their own suits."

Staying up all night making their own suits, getting good grades in school, staying out of trouble in the 'hood; all of these behaviors and characteristics, learned at a young age, are what mold the men and women in the Black masking tradition to live Indian when they're not dressed in their suit for Carnival. Learning the songs and how to throw signals, committing to practice and most of all to sewing, creates in these young ingenues a sacrificial discipline and humility that carries with them through adulthood. It is, as Fred Johnson said, "like a drug addiction. You can't get it out of you," but it is one with only positive reinforcements and attributes. It is a habit, an addictive behavior, you don't mind being passed through the bloodline, because that is the only way the culture continues. From generation to generation, each one paying tribute to a time before, to a century before, to ancestors before, in the actions and overall comportment practiced now and passed on to those born of your body and those who lay claim to it by your very presence in their environs.

Even for those who claim to not know what's next for the Mardi Gras Indian culture at large, like Romeo Bougere, his claim is spurious, tongue-in-cheek at best, when, in the next breath, he said, "If you ask for the future of us [9th Ward Hunters], it's them." Pride was evident in his voice as he pointed at his cousin still sitting patiently at the sewing table waiting for the interview to conclude.

"It's them." The "them" being children, cousins, nieces, nephews, neighborhood kids, or even students who become mesmerized by the Big Chief, or Flag Boy, or Second Chief who lives on or around their block. It is the community that helps to keep the culture going and moving forward even when its participants feel they no longer have the heart; when they no longer want to live Indian. In the public's appetite for the mystique, mirth, and magic that Black masking Indians bring year after year, a feedback loop is created that cycles the transference of energy and power from Indian to community and community to Indian. It is as strong and similar to the cyclical and codependent relationship that man has with God and in turn God has with man.

The spirit of those who came before, who masked before, is always present in the drumbeat, the shake of the tambourine, the dance, and the call of "Mardi cu de Fi O" before singing "Indian Red." They, too, are part of the community that fuels Indian culture and the Indians themselves. "I feel just drawn to be a part of something that's both ancient and contemporary and that is rooted in the mitochondria and the marrow of my bones," Cherice Harrison Nelson said.

She believes masking Indian is more than just a culture; rather, it is a calling that you have to do, a way of life one has to live: "It's very hard to ignore the call . . . to fulfill that almost biological need because without doing it, it affects me physically, affects the core of my being as a human." In answering that call, she, too, is living Indian, just like Romeo Bougere, Bo Dollis Jr., Stafford Agee, Keelian Boyd, Charles DuVernay, Ronnel Butler, and even, in his grief, Gilbert "Cosmo" Dave. They are living their lives in a way that is beyond merely participating in a cultural practice. Instead, they are disciplined in a spiritual practice, Harrison Nelson said: "It's a way of being. It's a way of living. It's a way of surviving."

Aerial view of UNO East Campus, New Orleans, after the flooding following Hurricane Katrina. Courtesy Louisiana & Special Collections, Earl K. Long Library, University of New Orleans.

4

Surviving Crisis and Chaos

Since their inception, the colony of La Louisiane and the city of New Orleans have been no strangers to hardship. Famine and raids by Indigenous tribes marked the crises during the beginning of the city's history. The Americans who flooded into the city after the Louisiana Purchase along with their strict social rules of caste, placement, ranking, and hierarchy policed the *gens de couleur libres* in a way they had never before experienced in the nineteenth century. Twentieth-century perils included hurricanes and a police strike in 1976 that directly impacted the parade culture of Black masking Indians, but in the long view of history, none of these growing pains seem to have been as detrimental to the city's Black Carnival celebrants, participants, and culture makers as Hurricane Katrina in 2005 and the scourge of the COVID-19 global pandemic that silently first rocked the unsuspecting city around Mardi Gras Day 2020.

KATRINA

Hurricane Katrina slammed the city of New Orleans on August 29, 2005, at Category 3 strength with sustained winds of 125 miles per hour. The powerful storm overwhelmed the city's weak flood protection system with fifty-three breaches where in some places the levee constituted only a high mound of dirt and grass that was supposed to keep people safe from walls of water they could not escape. What followed the storm was one of the worst floods the city had ever seen, with flooding in 80 percent of the city triggering a humanitarian crisis and the desperate need of American citizens—mostly Black—to evacuate. Some escaped days before the storm in cars; others were rescued in the hours and days after from rooftops by the Coast Guard or Cajun Navy. Others who evacuated to supposedly safe spaces such as the Convention Center and the Superdome needed to be evacuated again when conditions in those holding areas deteriorated with the storm and every passing day thereafter. What was left behind at the end of hurricane season 2005 was a city ravaged by water—specifically, the village of the Lower Ninth Ward, which some twenty thousand mostly Black, working-class families called home. Yet, this was not the only area that saw damage from the water, the mud, and the muck. In the scramble to "never let a good crisis go to waste"—the oft-quoted Winston Churchill remark espoused throughout the Katrina recovery period—plans were made, remade, and made over again about exactly what the city of New Orleans would and should look like.

New Orleans had been a majority-Black city since nearly its founding. Those dynamics and racial demographics did not change much over the course of the city's 287 years preceding Hurricane Katrina. After the storm, however, conversations about the city's future makeup were intense at the local, state, and federal levels. In the city itself, Mayor Ray Nagin established the Bring New Orleans Back Commission. A local developer, Pres Kabacoff, was one of the commission's seventeen members and had a penchant for saying in the media post-Katrina that he wanted to build a "smaller, taller" city. This comment, in addition to the persistent narrative that many of the flooded areas should be reverted back to the marshland and swamps they once were, came as an affront to the city's Black community—even those who remained displaced—because they heard the dog whistle in the political rhetoric and knew that what was really being said without being spoken was, *The city will be rich and white.* In the community of Black masking Indians, the comments instigated and agitated the spirit of resistance the Indians were founded upon.

"You know, again, with Katrina, they were talking about the city being all white," Darryl Montana said toward the end of the documentary *Tootie's Last Suit.* "You know I mask. I say, 'my family done put all this . . . the work that we do as it relates to the Mardi Gras Indian thing. You know, killing ourselves, doing this, keeping this thing going, and now you saying you don't want us back. You don't even want us back in the city?'"

"Nothing cancels Mardi Gras," Mayor Nagin said regarding the Carnival festivities in 2006. He led the Zulu parade down St. Charles Avenue that year. Yet in the back o' town and across the canal in the Black communities, his message rang loud and clear as Black masking Indians emerged from homes, some still under reconstruction, to mask in the spirit of defiance and resilience against the narrative that their people were unwanted and their culture had served its purpose and been dismissed.

Victor Harris, Big Chief of the Spirit of the Fi Yi Yi, started his tribe in 1984 after masking for years as the Flag Boy with the Yellow Pocahontas under Tootie Montana. His tribe dresses in suits with full facial masks, reminiscent of the masked egun in African Traditional Religions, in tribute and homage to the African roots of the masking tradition. On Carnival day in 2006, in a kelly-green suit of feathers, raffia, and a beaded mask, Harris declared over the roar of drums, singing, tambourines, and beating bells: "We got to make a stand! We gotta let 'em know! We're people. We are people!"

That Harris repeatedly declared, "We are people" among his tribe and the second line of community members against a backdrop of flooded-out and gutted homes is akin to the declarations that Black people in the United States, especially in the South, have been making since 1619. That Black people are, in fact, people, genus human. They are people who have homes, communities, cultures, social and familial ties to places that cannot be taken away, erased, or destroyed by violent acts of God. It is the message the first organized band of Black masking Indians sent in the mid- to late nineteenth century in the midst of Reconstruction, at its end, and at the beginning of Jim Crow. It is the message they sent in 2006 in the face of communal and cultural erasure because the act of restoring their humanity seemed too great a task even though they were heavily involved and committed to restoring themselves.

"The city came back," Keelian Boyd said about the 2006 Carnival season. "That was, that was big for me because I actually came in to get the bodies and all that." After the storm, Boyd worked as part of a search-and-rescue crew going through homes hoping to find the living, only to discover the dead: "It made me realize how important life really is. When you got kids and you done put babies in body bags . . . It had me in a bad state some days; some days good, some days bad."

After all he'd seen in helping during the storm recovery, he dressed his two-year-old son in an Indian suit for 2006 and let him mask for Mardi Gras. But it wasn't a traditional Mardi Gras Day for the gangs of Black masking Indians. "Indians wasn't even trying to meet," Bo Dollis Jr. said, recalling the time. "You know we had our suits on, but it was more to the point of we were glad that you was okay. I saw so many people crying." Dollis dubs the 2006 masking season as an experience he will never forget. Parading through the street out of tradition and duty yet swept up in the feeling of loss as he observed the destruction and then remembered the people he knew who had lived in those homes he passed. "They had one Indian, he had his suit hanging outside the house soaking wet and mildew and stuff like that, and I'm like, 'I wonder if he's alive or he's dead because they got his suit just hanging up outside.'"

In the Donald Harrison Collection at the Amistad Research Center at Tulane University there are photographs from October 24, 2005. One photograph depicts the exterior of the house with pink, waterlogged, beaded moccasins nailed to the blue paneling. The photographs show evidence of Indian living. Among the ruins was a blue-and-white three-spool sewing machine. Hot-pink thread had been pulled through the hooks, and the needles were poised to pounce on fabric to sew and create another suit. Pieces of that suit, or an older one, were also pulled from the wreckage of the home, including parts of an apron with beads in circular patches to match the moccasins along with framed pictures of Donald Harrison Jr. outside the door.

Of that time Cherice Harrison Nelson said: "I didn't dress 2006, my brother did. You know, it was very emotional, we were luckily able to save some things. Not everything." Ahead of the storm, members of the Harrison family put their Indian suits in the trunk of a car and parked that car in a lot downtown. After the storm, Lieutenant Governor Mitch Landrieu arranged for Herreast Harrison, the matriarch of the family, to be escorted into the city to retrieve their cars and their suits. "The suits were okay," Harrison Nelson said. "That was a wonderful thing to see."

Not everyone in the tradition was as fortunate as the Harrison family in being able to store their suits in a safe place during the storm, mostly because they didn't know what to expect. In 2005, there were few who were still active in the masking tradition who were old enough to have experienced Billion-Dollar Betsy forty years prior, which flooded the city of New Orleans. Most did not have that lived experience to prepare for Katrina.

"You know what I brought? A patch. No lie," Romeo Bougere said about what he packed when he finally evacuated the city in anticipation of Katrina. Quickly realizing that all he owned were the things he had with him, Bougere beaded his patch while displaced, and when he was finally allowed back in the city, he found another he could possibly wear: "The house was all flooded. When I walked through the door and kicked the door in, they had a patch, which was my dad's patch . . . it was still together and I took it. I took it and in 2006 that's what I wore."

The experience has not left him or his fellow Chief and 79rs Gang partner, Big Chief Jermaine Bossier of the 7th Ward Creole Hunters. On their 2020 album, *Expect the Unexpected,* Bougere and Bossier have a song called "Stop the Water" all about their Katrina experience set to the Mardi Gras Indian, "bamboula" beat, with the call-and-response chant characteristic of traditional Indian songs.

"When Katrina hit, nobody gave the outside people a real vision of what we went through in this storm shit," Bougere said. "The people who was displaced, the people who had to go here, who had to go here . . . like who lost shit, man, nobody ain't give you a good vision of what was going on." In his view of the lack of authentic experiences recorded about what really happened during Katrina, Bougere said he decided he would make a song "that put you in that motherfucking place."

He sang:

> They had a storm in the Gulf, I thought it was a joke
> Until I heard on the news that the levee broke.
> First time in my life I witnessed a storm,
> Put half of New Orleans in that Super Dome.
> That water kept rising and rising and did not stop,
> That water had my city, it was covered to the top.

People lived in that shelter for quite a few days,
And then the helicopter came and they was on they way.
Oh lord, Oh lord, this what the elders say.
They said let's all gather hands bow your heads and pray.

The song even details Bossier's experience of walking through the floodwater to check on his mother's house, only to find a note on the table telling him that she made it out.

For many of today's young, popular Indians who didn't experience the Jim Crow segregation the culture was forged in and the violence that fortified it, Hurricane Katrina was their first introduction to the perilous outside forces that could converge in an effort to cancel a culture bigger and beyond the people who participate in and contribute to it. In some opinions, Katrina made Indian culture bigger than it was before.

"I'm a be honest, though," Bougere began excitedly, "People was so happy to be back home, St. Joseph's Night for 2006, that bitch was jumping . . . Because you had people trying to come back you know."

Bo Dollis Jr. echoed a similar sentiment: "It just got bigger and bigger because a lot of people kept saying, 'New Orleans ain't gon' be,' 'Never again,' and 'It ain't gon' come back,' and stuff like that . . . and it came back stronger."

"Stronger." That's the way Gilbert "Cosmo" Dave described his best friend, Ronald W. Lewis, after Katrina; stronger. Lewis dedicated his life to preserving Black cultural traditions in New Orleans through his work at his museum, the House of Dance and Feathers, run out of workshops in his yard on Tupelo Street in the Lower Ninth Ward.

His home and museum were near-casualties of Katrina's wrath. "Hurricane Betsy in 1965 and Hurricane Katrina in 2005. I call them the two black holes in my life," Ronald wrote in his book named after his museum that documents his life and his work.

Ronald, who had lived through the flooding of Betsy as a boy, knew what it would take to rebuild his community. He returned to the city in October after evacuating to Thibodaux. When he saw his home still standing, he said to himself, "Well I have a chance." After attending a *ReInhabiting NOLA* meeting in November 2005 and garnering the help of dozens of volunteers, Ronald was able to elevate the work he'd already been doing and place the story of Katrina at the center of the evolving cultural traditions he was involved in.

In those early days of the recovery, journalists and reporters nearly outnumbered the people who were returning home to salvage what was left of their lives. Ronald used their platform and presence to his advantage, writing, "Once I got attuned to all the media, scholars, schools, and volunteer groups who were traveling through my neighborhood, I utilized those resources for the benefit of my community—putting that message out there, and letting it be known that the city wasn't gonna tear down our houses and turn our land into 'green space.'"

It was this determination that inspired some and made others question the determination of one man with a museum in his backyard. The late journalist Dan Baum, who died of brain cancer in 2020, was one of the reporters who questioned Ronald's conviction that his neighborhood was going to come back. Ronald took Baum to task for his depicting him as delusional. He said then, "Dan, you're a journalist, and you can't look and feel what I was feeling, and you did what a journalist do." Chastened, Ronald wrote that Baum took to calling him a prophet and even became an advocate for the Lower Ninth Ward himself because Baum saw "the spirit of the people of this Lower Ninth Ward."

As Victor Harris said months later on Mardi Gras Day in 2006, "The spirit was calling." The spirit of the ancestors—enslaved, free, and Indigenous. The spirit of tradition. The spirit of community, of culture, of togetherness, of masking Indian once again. This spirit was present in the people who dressed out that year—just six months after the storm—and in their second line of support. They marched among the ruins of lives and livelihoods, bringing beauty to neighborhoods both desolate and decimated, vowing in their presence the creed of their most sacred song, "we won't bow down." Staunch in their conviction then that the culture is what brings the people back, it would be the collision course of the culture and the crush of people gathered together to celebrate Mardi Gras, in all its ways, that would present the deadliest threat to the evolved tradition that has come to represent resistance, rebellion, and resilience.

COVID-19

The first confirmed case of SARS-CoV-2—the 2019 novel coronavirus that causes the COVID-19 infection—in the United States was on January 21, 2020. A Washington state resident had returned from Wuhan, China, on January 15 and tested positive. The World Health Organization (WHO) labeled COVID-19 a global health emergency on January 31. The Trump administration declared a nationwide public health emergency on February 3. On March 11, the WHO declared COVID-19 a global pandemic. The Trump administration declared COVID-19 a national emergency two days later. Between the time of the first positive case in the country and the declaration of a national emergency, Carnival season in the city of New Orleans had come and gone. The Feast of the Epiphany kicked off the season on January 6, which concluded with Mardi Gras on February 25. The annual culminating event brought more than a million people to the Crescent City. One month later, Mardi Gras was deemed a superspreader event that was responsible for nearly half of the state's COVID cases and deaths at the time.

Among those deaths was that of Ronald W. Lewis. The founder of the Choctaw Hunters Mardi Gras Indian tribe. The founder of the Big 9 Social Aid & Pleasure Club. The Gatekeeper for the North Side Skull and Bones Gang. The uncle of this author's cousin. Lewis was hospitalized and tested for COVID-19 on March 18. That's just nine days after the first positive case of COVID was identified in the entire state of Louisiana. Lewis died, two days later, on March 20, at the age of sixty-eight.

"The loss is a big loss," Gilbert "Cosmo" Dave said about Ronald's death. "I could say so many things, but my heart right now, just talking about him I'm still a little bit emotional and sad about it, but I know I gotta bounce back for him and for the culture, you know what I'm saying."

The day Cosmo opened up his heart about his life, the life of his friend Ronald W. Lewis, and the masking tradition was one day before a second-line parade was to be held in Lewis's honor. The parade in early July came more than four months after Lewis's death, when, in the midst of the COVID outbreak in the city, gatherings of more than ten people were prohibited in New Orleans.

Still, his legacy loomed as large as his loss. Although his wife, Charlotte "Minnie" Hill, was too wracked with grief to discuss her husband and his work, she did allow me access to the museum that had been shuttered since Ronald's death. Inside the crowded and hot workshops were mementos and memorabilia embedded with beauty and majesty as well as testaments to his contribution to the culture. Among the items was a thank-you note from President Obama that read: "We would like to extend our deepest thanks and appreciation for your generous gift. It is gratifying to know that we have your support. As we work to address the great challenges of our time, we hope you will continue to stay active and involved. Again thanks for your kind gift."

Headdresses in every color, beaded, and fully feathered adorned the walls and display tables along with wooden masks, and books. There were pictures of Ronald with actor Wendell Pierce and activist and politician Julian Bond. Stacks of CDs, felt hats that had seen their better years—most likely from Ronald's parades with the Big 9 Social Aid & Pleasure Club—and certificates of honor from the Choctaw Hunters, mayoral recognition, and more. Inside the museum it is clear that Ronald Lewis provided the dance, the jazz, the music, sound, and heart of the community. As Cosmo said about his friendship and work with Ronald, "We do it from the heart."

Working from the heart is what kept Black masking Indians going as the COVID way of life set in for them shortly after Mardi Gras. Their festivities for St. Joseph's Night and Super Sunday were canceled. Jazz Fest was canceled. The Indians wore their suits only once in 2020, and yet most were all sewing on a new suit for 2021, only to have the mayor cancel Mardi Gras, shut down bars, and ban liquor sales in the French Quarter to prevent a repeat of the prior year's Mardi Gras COVID superspreader event.

"If they don't have a Mardi Gras next year, I think it'll be just like another Katrina; everybody'll just be so glad to see each other," Bo Dollis Jr. said, projecting into the future. "With the pandemic, everybody is knowing who's passing away. I've known so many people that's passed away from the pandemic, you know, especially as far as entertainers, musicians, just friends outside of it [from] regular life."

Legendary jazz pianist Ellis Marsalis, patriarch of the Marsalis musical family, died from COVID-19 at age eighty-five. Theresa Elloie, who hosted Mardi Gras Indians at Sportsman's Corner bar in Central City, died from COVID-19; she was sixty-three. But even deaths not related to COVID hit the Indian community just as hard. Guardians of the Flame Counsel Chief Joseph Jenkins died at age ninety. He had been in hospice care at the time of his death on April 16, 2020. He was believed to be the oldest living Indian and had built a new suit every year from the time he first started masking in 1955 with the Seminoles until 2016, when his vision failed him.

Although Jenkins was sent home with a small burial ceremony after his death in April, a larger memorial service was planned for what would have been his ninety-first birthday on July 14, 2020. Cherice Harrison Nelson planned the event. "It was really difficult having a life celebration during a pandemic," she said. The service was held at the New Orleans Jazz Museum and live-streamed to an audience of eight thousand. "It was important to have his celebration because I think in some way people live for their life celebration," Harrison Nelson said. "How do you have the funerary rites so closely tied to this tradition during a pandemic?" Harrison Nelson kept Jenkins in mind as she meticulously planned different portions of the service to include African tradition, Indian tradition, and Christian tradition. "He had an expression that he would say," Harrison Nelson began, before mimicking Jenkins, "'You did that. You did that, Baby.' And everything I did, I planned it so he would say that."

For those the pandemic didn't take, life has still been an adjustment. Romeo Bougere, who works for the city, began being tested regularly after the virus spread in New Orleans. However, he believed he contracted COVID shortly after Mardi Gras, though he was never tested to confirm his suspicions.

"Everybody that I know that I've ever been around, they was sick right after Mardi Gras," Bougere said. "I was sicker than I've ever been before in my life. It felt like my back . . . no taste, I couldn't breathe, my mouth, respiratory." He said he went to a clinic to get checked out and was told he didn't have anything. "So, I'm telling you how I feel, and you gon' tell me I ain't got nothing," Bougere exclaimed in anger.

Though he didn't mask for 2020, he was still beading a new patch. "I'm only sewing because I don't have a choice," he said, explaining his work as a way to pass the endless hours that constitute time in the pandemic.

Sewing remained the one constant for most of the Indians even amid their fears and concerns about COVID and the future of their cultural traditions. "I've been a musician for thirty-seven years, and I haven't had to have a job in thirty-seven years until this pandemic, so now I'm focusing on just being prepared for life," Stafford Agee said when asked if he was sewing in the middle of a pandemic. While he didn't explicitly say he wasn't sewing, it was evident that he longed to mask. "I don't want to be heartbroken by sewing a suit and can't put it on because I don't believe this is an overnight thing."

Shawmika Boyd, wife of Keelian Boyd, and Big Queen of the Young Maasai Hunters, agreed with Agee that the pandemic and the restrictions it imposed weren't going to end. "I don't think COVID is going anywhere, anytime soon," she said. "We don't have to keep missing out on the things that we normally do in terms of seeing that [Mardi Gras Indians]." Boyd suggested the Indians and all of Mardi Gras go virtual for 2021, which happened with the three-day streaming event "Mardi Gras for All Y'all."

"The spirit hit us today," said Jeremy Stevenson, Second Chief Lil' Pi for the Monogram Hunters Indian tribe, on the first night of the streaming celebration. Taped in advance of Carnival, the Monogram Hunters gathered in an open field with their drums and tambourines and sang traditional Indian songs like "Golden Crown" and "Jockomo." The footage was spliced with members of various tribes marching in their suits including Yellow Pocahontas, Wild Apache, Creole Wild West, Wild Magnolia, Golden Eagles, and more. In the segment, featuring the Indians, they discussed their history, the feeling of masking, and what it means to continue their culture despite the ravages of COVID. "It's refreshing to be able to put on your suit and have that camaraderie with other members of the nation," Second Chief Joseph Boudreaux of the Golden Eagles said during the streaming event.

In shiny, new beaded suits, uptown and downtown Indians came together to present their history, legacy, and future in a different way. "It's very sacred," said Tyrone Stevenson, Chief Pi of the Monogram Hunters about the meaning of Mardi Gras Indians: "It's our way of releasing the spirits of the Indian nation of all the people that came before us and gone now." In releasing the spirits in a digital environment, the Indians who participated in the streaming celebration brought their culture to nearly one hundred thousand different viewers by Mardi Gras Day 2021, with a viewership that would only grow over the coming days, weeks, months, and years. Just as the story of those first dancing Indigenous tribes and Africans in Congo Square are preserved in antebellum memoirs and newspaper accounts, so, too, is the current history of these tribes of Black masking Indians. They continue to tell their story and to leave a legacy for those coming behind them in the future to build on.

THE FUTURE OF THE CULTURE

The mysteries of the Mardi Gras Indians have been peeled back with every successive generation. Much of that is due to the sheer intrigue the Indians inspire when journalists, writers, and filmmakers learn of or are introduced to this community of Black men, women, and children who lead otherwise normal, unspectacular lives but create beauty in their spare time to participate in a tradition that goes back to the beginnings of their ancestral homeland. This inspired intrigue in storytellers has created what's become known as the third line.

The Indians are first, their followers the second line, the reporters, journalists, and authors the third.

However, as the desire for Indian culture and the need to preserve its history increased throughout the twentieth century, Indians themselves found a way to participate in their own study. "The commercial thing is more prevalent than the natural thing . . . Everybody is out there for the Yankee dollar," Big Chief Donald Harrison Sr. told biographer Al Kennedy.

During his life, Donald Harrison Sr. participated in opening up the culture of Black masking Indians to those who would have never encountered it, touring across the country at festivals in Fort Lauderdale, Houston, and even the "Gathering of Nations" in New Mexico—a powwow that included more than five hundred Indigenous tribes from the United States and Canada—as well as traveling internationally in Martinique, Italy, France, and other countries in Europe. Harrison and his family also traveled to Yale University in 1995 to honor the first woman to be elected Principal Chief of the Cherokee Nation, Wilma Mankiller, as part of the Chubb Fellowship Award Ceremony.

The spread of the culture of Mardi Gras Indians continues through Herreast Harrison and the Guardians Institute, where they've given away forty thousand books to schoolchildren in New Orleans. "We go into the schools and we present books to, at minimum, a grade level, and we include a cultural presentation and a reading of the book," Cherice Harrison Nelson said about the work she continues with her mother and tribe.

Many of the Indians go into schools and do presentations for children in addition to holding their own cultural events in the community. However, one way the culture and traditions of Black masking Indians have spread the fastest has been through Indian music. Bo Dollis Sr. made many albums with his tribe, the Wild Magnolias, after attending a White Eagles Indian practice and meeting Quinton Davis, who ran Jazz Fest. Bo Dollis Jr. recounted the story, saying Davis heard his father sing and then said: "Well who is this guy? You know we gotta get him in the studio." From the albums came a new, popular Indian song, "Handa Wanda," and a more traditional song, "Fiyah Water." "Half the songs that we hearing today is his traditional songs that he made all over the world," Bo Dollis Jr. said.

Bo has continued what his father started, using the music he now makes with the Wild Magnolias to spread Indian culture far and wide. He supports the commercialization of the tradition he loves. "Mardi Gras Indians has been so much in the shell for so long," he said. He advocates for a Mardi Gras Indian ball or even a Mardi Gras Indian picnic to further spread the work and history of Black masking Indians.

But not everyone supports the commercialized spread of the culture. Journalist and author Sarah M. Broom noted in her memoir, *The Yellow House,* that there was something crass about how Mardi Gras Indians were seemingly pimped out on the streets to promote tourism. Of her time living in the French Quarter in the 2010s, she wrote, "The Black Indian wearing a dirty purple suit, posing on the edge of my block for photographs with a Home Depot tip bucket hidden behind his feathers, feels like a transgression." She went on to note the sacred culture of Black masking Indians and how rarely they're seen in their suits before remarking in seeming disgust, "But now, you can be photographed with a man dressing up as one [an

Indian] for a dollar, at your command." Whether this culture is spread through events where Indians are hired to add hometown charm to the atmosphere, to record deals, books (including this one), documentaries, movies, TV shows and more. Michael P. Smith noted the sometimes predatory nature of these commercial opportunities in his 1994 book *Mardi Gras Indians:*

> A cherished activity, essentially a religious activity, pursued in private spaces and isolated neighborhoods for more than a century, has been thrown into a strange new public marketplace. Art collectors, record producers, music managers, and other entrepreneurs see the Indian gangs as an economic opportunity . . . Especially confusing is the "role" of outside documentarians and folklorists (black and white) who now frequent the community. How does one distinguish between fellow artists and supporters and commercial entrepreneurs who take and run, giving nothing back to the community?

There is a term for those commercial entrepreneurs who take without giving back to the community: culture vultures. Romeo Bougere was hesitant to participate in the interview for this book because he was concerned about how his culture was going to be portrayed and what the author would be receiving monetarily that would never come to him to support him as a man, a husband, a father, and as an Indian who regularly gives back to the tradition he's grown up in. He and his recording partner made a song of that same name where they express their frustrations and grievances against those who are clout chasing and looking to capitalize off of their cultural contributions.

Way in the morning
They strike without warning
They strike without reason
When it's Indian season

Come walk take a picture
They trying to get wit' ya
Say here, here's a look
Come pose for my book

But they do it so wrong
Because they don't want to go home

I'm chief, your devotion
I got mixed emotions
I might feel sad
Sometimes I feel mad
Never do I feel glad
Never do I feel glad
I'm chief going ham
Don't wanna teach their program
Don't wanna teach their program

They like our chants
Then apply for our grants
Say come milk the gang

I wish they never came
But who can I blame

Ooh way in the evenin'
Ooh way in the evenin'
It's exposing season
They done gave me a reason
To shine a light
Hope it shine, shine, shine bright
Culture Vulture

Despite his misgivings about the intent of this project, Bougere, once the interview began, spoke at length about being a Black masking Indian and his burgeoning music career. "I swear to God, I love this shit!," he exclaimed more than once. "I'm talking about all day long I'm singing this shit." It is in his singing and his storytelling that he continues to contribute and expand the access outsiders have to the tradition of Black masking Indians. His joy, his pride, and his love for all things Indian is infectious and ebullient. "I ain't masking Mardi Gras Indian for the culture. I ain't choose the culture, the culture chose me," he said. Yet he chose it right back, even if at first, as a boy, he did so begrudgingly. As a man, he knows there is nothing else he would rather do. "I'm doing it for me because when I put this motherfucker on there," he said pointing to his half-beaded patch, "there is no better feeling in the world."

Romeo's pride in his work, his music, and the culture gives elders like Gilbert "Cosmo" Dave the satisfaction of knowing that what he loved as a little boy will continue for little boys for generations to come. "The bead work they do, the big-sized aprons, they got four, five pieces on," Dave said. "They don't need all that from my understanding, I don't like all that, but that's how they doing it now. They are not playing. They took it to another level."

With each successive generation, the culture of Black masking Indians has innovated and evolved, be it in beading style, the types of feathers used, the songs sung, the construction of a crown, or any other small nuance that has adapted over time. As an Indigenous, cultural, and spiritual tradition, Black masking Indians are the embodiment of a living, breathing organism, a historical legacy that will ebb, flow, and change with the cultural, socioeconomic, and racial conditions of the time. As Cherice Harrison Nelson said: "I still think that the future people will find new ways to do what they do. I don't think it's dead."

Rooted in rebellion and resistance, the fight for Black men to be seen as men, and Black people to be seen as people, the Mardi Gras Indians gave and continue to give their communities dignity and joy at Carnival and all throughout the year. "It's not gon' never end," Cosmo said. "This is a street parade, this is our parade. You don't see us walking behind no floats on Mardi Gras. You never seen us on Canal Street . . . It started years [ago] and way before I was born, it's been Mardi Gras Indians. It's our thing, Baby. It's for us and it ain't gon' never end. It's not gon' ever end because you got the little boys coming up, and they growing up to be men, and they gon' make it keep on going . . . Trust me."

With more than five hundred years of history to point to between Africa, Europe, and America, the culture of Black masking Indians seems poised to stand another five hundred years—if not more than that—of beading, singing, dancing, rebelling, and resisting, in their beauty that's never been bowed.

Conclusion

"Nobody ain't never gonna find the code," the late Big Chief Larry Bannock of the Golden Star Hunters said during an interview at Jazz Fest in 1991. The code he was talking about included all the unique origins of the Mardi Gras Indians. Although we know the origins are both Indigenous and African, European and Catholic, it is not the origin story that is the most important. It is the evolution of Black masking Indians that is most intriguing. The continued growth and maturation of the Mardi Gras Indians is part history lesson and part urban legend, all mixing into one to add even more mystery the more corroborated information you find. It is magical and true, fantastical and real. The more you know, the more you realize you don't know and may never know because the history is too long, the stories too old, and most of their tellers are now ancestors.

The *sangamentos* and warrior culture of the Kongolese live on. The procession culture of Catholic missionaries lives on, along with their play *Moors and Christians.* The syncretized African Traditional Religions that produced Ifá, Candomblé, Santería, Lucumi, and Vodun live on. The calumet ceremonies of Indigenous tribes live on. All of it, the sacred and secular, profane and prophetic, can be observed in the masking of Black men, women and children as tribal plains Indians from a time gone by.

The culture survived the transatlantic slave trade, the Louisiana Purchase, the Indian Removal Act, Civil War, Reconstruction, Jim Crow, the civil rights movement, Hurricanes Betsy and Katrina, the latest racial reckoning brought on by Black Lives Matter, and the global pandemic that is COVID-19. In all of these tremors that have shaken the foundations of life, especially Black life, in New Orleans, the culture, tradition, and practices of Black masking Indians have remained constant and consistent.

A description of an 1838 Mardi Gras parade described people dressed as Harlequins, Turks, and Wild Indians. Another report eight years later took note of people "in a variety of costumes—some as Indians with feathers in their heads." Now the history is preserved on albums, streaming platforms like Tidal and YouTube, and in books spanning the decades, generations, and centuries. All of the research, every tidbit of information, every new link found between the contemporary and the ancient, each Indian willing to give an interview adds to the pantheon that has become the unbreakable, impervious, and evolutionary tradition of Black masking Indians.

acknowledgments

I have written many books, but this is my first nonfiction title (something that was never on my radar) and my first that is not self-published. It is only right, then, that the first thank-you goes to Jenny Keegan with LSU Press, who sent me that unsolicited email I mention in the preface, asking if I would be interested in writing what is now this book. Jenny, that email, and your belief in my work from a one-off essay about red beans and rice through shepherding this project through to publication, have restored a confidence in me that had been lost due to always ending up in the publishing industry's slush pile of rejection. I am forever grateful for you seeing me, and I hope this puts the rest of the industry on notice that I got something to say. LOL.

Next, I have to thank my family. My mom, for helping me with the proposal, driving with me to New Orleans in the middle of a GLOBAL PANDEMIC (we'd never seen the Quarter that empty, have we, Mommy?), and listening to me talk on and on about this book as I researched it and put it together. Mommy, your unwavering love and support are everything I need, have needed, will need, and more. I love you forever, and I thank you for always believing in my dreams and nurturing them to fruition.

I also have to thank my cousins L'Maun Morris, Tanya Devey, and Brent Taylor, who called their friends and threatened them into talking to me (Tanya), took me around the city and introduced me to folks (L'Maun), and gave me access to the culture in a way most outsiders never would have (all). I know I've always been far away, but you all have nevertheless always treated me like family, and for that I'm thankful.

There are loads more family and family friends who have helped me with this text in big and small ways. Thank you to my aunts Mary, Sharon, and Cynthia; my mother's best friend, Betty Nelson; my father, Ned Leeper; his friend Erroll Lebeau; and the lady at Amistad Research Center who was patient with me as I went through the Harrison family archive donations at closing time and still made my copies even though it was her quitting time.

The biggest thanks go to the Black masking Indians themselves. Stafford Agee, Bo Dollis Jr., Romeo Bougere, Cherice Harrison Nelson, Ronnel Butler, Gilbert "Cosmo" Dave, Charles Duvernay, Jennie Wimbish, Shawmika Edwards Boyd, and the late Keelian Boyd. Thank you to you all for opening your hearts. To those I met in person, thank you for opening your homes. Thank you for being patient with me as I asked my questions like a true intrigued outsider and for giving me real and thoughtful answers. I hope you see this work as a labor of love, meant to help further spread and promote the culture with respect for your artistry, your humanity, and your history. And to the ancestors, both in and out of the tradition, who have guided me to this point in my work, who woke me out of my sleep with words when I doubted that I would even be able to write this book, and who continue to guide me in the right direction, I give thanks. Asé.

Finally, I'd like to thank my children: Mylen, who was down for the ride to New Orleans and whom I dragged through archives and museums on our "research vacation" (I know I owe you some beignets), and my daughter, Annelise, whom I was pregnant with as I wrote the first draft of this text, who was only months old as I revised, and will be one by the time the book is out. Baby Girl, if you ever read this, I hope it shows you better than I can tell you that it is possible to do all things, have all things, and be all things. There's magic in you!

And to my husband, Jermaine, you bet on me when I barely wanted to bet on myself. It hasn't been easy, but I thank you for your trust in my gift, in my words, and in my work. Thank you.

notes

Introduction

2 "The blending of African, European, and Native American": Eric Waters (photographs) and Karen Celestan (narrative), *Freedom's Dance: Social Aid and Pleasure Clubs in New Orleans* (Baton Rouge: Louisiana State University Press, 2018), 138.

3 "the northern periphery": Jeroen Dewulf, *From the Kingdom of Kongo to Congo Square: Kongo Dances and the Origins of the Mardi Gras Indians* (Lafayette: University of Louisiana at Lafayette Press, 2017), xx.

3 "are not a uniquely Louisianian product": Dewulf, xiii.

5 "the deepest sense of connection": Shane Lief and John McCusker, *Jockomo: The Native Roots of Mardi Gras Indians* (Jackson: University Press of Mississippi, 2019), 3.

1. In the Beginning Was the World

8 "a complex web of activities": Lief and McCusker, 3.

10 "What I remember about parades": *Tootie's Last Suit*, dir. Lisa Katzman, 2009.

10 "I never experienced the white Carnival": *Tootie's Last Suit.*

12 "rebelling and liberating themselves": Christian Scott (christianscottofficial), "Happy Indigenous Peoples Day. Chief Adjuah—Chieftain and Idi of the Xodokan Nation. Black Tribes of New Orleans. Black Indians of New Orleans are Louisiana based West African tribal Chiefdoms," Instagram, October 12, 2020, https://www.instagram com/p/CGP7vMsHI0V/.

13 That work was completed by 1491: Dewulf, 24.

13 "[They] were well aware": Dewulf, 30.

13 “*Sangamento* is derived from”: Cécile Fromont, *The Art of Conversion: Christian Visual Culture in the Kingdom of Kongo* (Chapel Hill: University of North Carolina Press, 2014), 21.

13 “would typically wear”: Dewulf, 23.

15 There are many evolutionary steps: For more information on how the Portuguese converted the Kingdom of Kongo through the syncretism of Catholicism with Kongolese spiritual and ritual traditions using the Catholic play *Moors and Christians* and through Catholic Brotherhood societies that devolved into secret fraternal orders and mutual aid groups of which the Mardi Gras Indians exemplify, see Dewulf.

15 Now the Kingdom of Kongo: Dewulf, 27.

15 “election ceremonies”: Dewulf, 29.

16 “only fragmentary traces”: Lief and McCusker, 28.

16 “people of African descent”: Mary Elliott and Jazmine Hughes, “No. 1 / Slavery, Power and the Human Cost,” *New York Times: The 1619 Project,* August 18, 2019, 4.

16–17 This sixteenth-century presence: Dewulf, 1.

17 “village of the blacks”: Pierre Le Moyne d’Iberville, *Iberville’s Gulf Journals (1698–1702),* trans. and ed. Richebourg Gaillard McWilliams (Tuscaloosa: University of Alabama Press, 1991), 154.

17 As noted in the 2003 documentary: *All on a Mardi Gras Day,* dir. Royce Osborn, 2003, https://www.kweli.tv/programs/all-on-a-mardi-gras-day.

17 Therefore these “Black Indians”: *The Black Indians of New Orleans,* dir. Maurice Martinez, 1976, Amistad Research Center.

18 “was both a superhighway”: Lief and McCusker, 27.

18 One such ceremony took place: Lief and McCusker, 30–33.

18 “The musical procession in New Orleans”: Lief and McCusker, 32.

19 “the Natchez had annihilated”: Lief and McCusker, 37–39.

19 “Don’t stop! Just keep going!”: Al Kennedy, *Big Chief Harrison and the Mardi Gras Indians* (Gretna, LA: Pelican, 2010), 163.

20 “For twenty years or more”: Jerah Johnson, *Congo Square in New Orleans* (New Orleans: Louisiana Landmarks Society, 1995), 5.

20 “Starting in 1719”: Dewulf, 1–2.

21 “In many cases [the planters]”: Johnson, 5–6.

21 intermixing between Indigenous tribes and Africans: Johnson, 11.

22 “Louis is more Indian”: *Daily Delta* (New Orleans), May 21, 1853, 6.

22 “TWENTY FIVE DOLLARS REWARD”: *Daily Picayune* (New Orleans), December 10, 1850, 4.

23 “On the outskirts of New Orleans”: Daniel H. Usner, *American Indians in Early New Orleans: From Calumet to Raquette* (Baton Rouge: LSU Press, 2018), 171.

23 The ruling allowed European: "John Marshall and Supreme Court of the United States," *U.S. Reports: Johnson v. McIntosh, 21 U.S. 8 Wheat. 543,* 1823, periodical, retrieved from the Library of Congress, www.loc.gov/item/usrep021543/.

24 "You had Indians who were still living": *Tootie's Last Suit.*

24 Federal laws in addition to state: Lief and McCusker, 42.

24 "Consequently, as the decades passed": Johnson, 11.

25 "Masters give their negroes": Jean-Francois-Benjamin Dumont de Montigny, *Mémoires historiques sur la Louisiane contenant ce qui y est arrivé de plus mémorable depuis l'année 1687, jusqu'á présent . . .* (Paris, 1753), translated as "History of Louisiana" in *Historical Collections of Louisiana,* comp. Benjamin F. French, 5 vols. (New York: Wiley and Putnam, 1846–53), 5:120.

26 "the trading activities of [the enslaved]": Johnson, 12.

26 "While African dances had been performed": Johnson, 37.

26 In his *Histoire de la Louisiane:* Dewulf, 2.

26 In 1799 a similar observation: Dewulf, 3–8.

27 During this encounter he noted: Benjamin Henry Boneval Latrobe, *Impressions Respecting New Orleans: Diary & Sketches 1818–1820,* ed. Samuel Wilson Jr. (New York: Columbia University Press, 1951), 49–51.

27 "I went to Ghana in 1999": *All on a Mardi Gras Day.*

28 Brown noted the largest group: William Wells Brown, *My Southern Home or, The South and Its People* (Boston: A. G. Brown, 1880), 121–24.

28 the Fulas (a nomadic people from West Africa): Dewulf, 10.

30 "Now you wanna get": *The Black Indians of New Orleans.*

30 "the Camp to share these ludicrous": Dewulf, 8–9.

30 "they continued to live in New Orleans": Lief and McCusker, 45.

30 "Congo Square is the first place": *Tootie's Last Suit.*

30 He also noted that it was: Johann Ulrich Buechler, *Land- und Seereisen eines St. Gallischen Kantonsbürgers nach Nordamerika und Westindien . . . in den Jahren 1816, 1817 und 1818, Etc.* (1820).

30 "by-product of the square's market function": Johnson, 5.

31 "The enslaved population having a degree of autonomy": Johnson, 8.

31 "While the city": Johnson, 19.

32 "Some were in red": Marc-Antoine Caillot, *A Company Man* (New Orleans: Historic New Orleans Collection, 2013), 135; Sophie White, "Massacre, Mardi Gras, and Torture in Early New Orleans," *William and Mary Quarterly,* 3rd ser., 70 (July 2013): 497–538.

33 "Such was the case when": Lief and McCusker, 82.

33 Mardi Gras did not make a resurgence: Robert Tallant, *Mardi Gras . . . As It Was* (Gretna, LA: Pelican, 1989), 100.

34 There were also "characters": Lief and McCusker, 83.

34 That they remained on the fringes: Lief and McCusker, 83–84.

35 Three Kings Day to Fat Tuesday: Dewulf, 135.

35 "theatrical rituals involving dancing": Dewulf, 98.

36 "no question that the origin": *Tootie's Last Suit.*

36 light the way for the Comus krewe: Dewulf, 136.

36–37 "Negroes have gone extensively": Dewulf, 137.

37 "At 3 p.m. yesterday": "Maskers Visit Algiers," *Daily Picayune (New Orleans),* February 27, 1895, 2.

38 Their resurgence in nineteenth-century pop culture: Lief and McCusker, 69, 91–92.

38 By 1870, the Indian: Lief and McCusker, 92.

38–39 "Among the revelers we observed": "Scenes from the Streets," *Times-Democrat (New Orleans),* February 22, 1871, 10.

39 This masked Indian: Lief and McCusker, 69, 46, 50.

40 "The Mistick Krewe of Comus, Twelfth Night Revelers": Lief and McCusker, 85.

41 "Who is there to stop me": Dewulf, 169–71.

41 In this way, the Mardi Gras Indians: Dewulf, 168.

42 "African culture in the New World": Johnson, 43.

2. Mardi Gras Indians Today

44 "My Daddy, according to my mother": *Tootie's Last Suit.*

44 "I just knew I was going to mask": Al Kennedy, *Chief of Chiefs: Robert Nathaniel Lee and the Mardi Gras Indians of New Orleans, 1915–2001* (Gretna, LA: Pelican, 2018), 33.

44 He came from a family that masked: Lief and McCusker, 132,

45 In 1929, at the age of thirteen: Kennedy, *Chief of Chiefs,* 59–62.

45 From that moment on, Harrison knew: Kennedy, *Big Chief Harrison,* 19–20.

45 This is despite the fact that two: Kennedy, *Big Chief Harrison,* 58, 27.

46 "Much consternation was caused when": "Maskers Visit Algiers," *Daily Picayune (New Orleans),* February 27, 1895, 2.

47 "Every Mardi Gras bunches of negroes": "The Coon Carnival," *Times-Democrat (New Orleans),* February 28, 1900.

48 While the paper said the fight: Kennedy, *Chief of Chiefs,* 33–34.

50 "I wanted them to have": Kennedy, *Big Chief Harrison,* 156–57.

50 Yvonne's fear was warranted: Kennedy, *Big Chief Harrison,* 157.

50 "They never go to church": Kennedy, *Big Chief Harrison,* 151.

51 "In the past, if a fellow wasn't rough": Kennedy, *Big Chief Harrison,* 149.

51 "he wasn't a better man": Kennedy, *Chief of Chiefs,* 34.

51 "They used to carry real shotguns": *The Black Indians of New Orleans.*

51–52 "I mean, he'd have it so you could stick": Kennedy, *Big Chief Harrison,* 153.
52 Big Chief Drew (Andrew Justin) remembered seeing: Kennedy, *Big Chief Harrison,* 151.
52 "It's a good song": Kennedy, *Big Chief Harrison,* 154.
52 (Shallow Water Oh Mama): *The Black Indians of New Orleans.*
54 Your Spy Boy eat raw pork chop: *Tootie's Last Suit.*
56 "The year I masked with him": *The Black Indians of New Orleans.*
56 "My Daddy was great in his way": *Tootie's Last Suit.*
56 "My Daddy, he never just sat me down": *Tootie's Last Suit.*
59 "Mimicking others, he said": *Tootie's Last Suit.*
62 "one of the greatest Indian sewers": Rachel Breunlin and Ronald W. Lewis, with essays by Helen Regis, *The House of Dance and Feathers: A Museum by Ronald W. Lewis* (New Orleans: UNO Press/Neighborhood Story Project, 2009), 107.
62 "I enjoy creating the suits": Breunlin and Lewis, 107.
67–68 "If you ever had the opportunity": *Guardians of the Flame: New Orleans Mardi Gras Indians,* 1993, Amistad Research Center.
68 "It was just like being in a religious service": *Guardians of the Flame: New Orleans Mardi Gras Indians.*
68 "It's just something that come over you": *Guardians of the Flame: New Orleans Mardi Gras Indians.*
70 "I swear he was pretty": Kennedy, *Big Chief Harrison,* 117.
74 "express the desire that I guard": *Guardians of the Flame: New Orleans Mardi Gras Indians.*
79 "I was born to mask with the Indians": Kennedy, *Big Chief Harrison,* 36.

3. Living Indian

85 "When he first started masking": *Tootie's Last Suit.*
85 "Tootie and I both had full-time jobs": *Tootie's Last Suit.*
86 "You can't be an Indian every day": *Tootie's Last Suit.*
86 that to be an Indian was to be "rough": Kennedy, *Big Chief Harrison,* 149.
88 "The reason I didn't mask": Qtd. in Kennedy, *Big Chief Harrison.*
88 "He did not like to have anyone": Kennedy, *Big Chief Harrison,* 267.
89 "I never said anything more": Kennedy, *Big Chief Harrison,* 170.
91 "that no bill collectors will be dunning": "Carnival," *Louisiana Weekly,* February 25, 1928, 6.
91 "make a suit, then get broke": Kennedy, *Chief of Chiefs,* 66–67.
95 blamed her brother's blindness later in life: Kennedy, *Chief of Chiefs,* 62.
99 "After I found out he accepted": Kennedy, *Chief of Chiefs,* 39.
99 "Brother Tillman welcomed children": Kennedy, *Chief of Chiefs,* 41.

100 “masked a few little times”: Breunlin and Lewis, 102–4.

101 “like a drug addiction”: Breunlin and Lewis, 73.

4. Surviving Crisis and Chaos

107 build a “smaller, taller” city: Gary Rivlin, *Katrina: After the Flood* (New York: Simon and Schuster, 2015), 137, 211.

107 “You know, again, with Katrina”: *Tootie’s Last Suit.*

108 “We got to make a stand!”: *Tootie’s Last Suit.*

113 “Hurricane Betsy in 1965”: Breunlin and Lewis, 45.

113 “Well I have a chance”: Breunlin and Lewis, 47.

113 Ronald used their platform: Breunlin and Lewis, 55.

114 “the spirit of the people”: Breunlin and Lewis, 55.

114 “The spirit was calling”: *Tootie’s Last Suit.*

115 Lewis died, two days later: Jordan Hirsch, “Stop Shaming New Orleans for Holding Mardi Gras,” *Slate,* April 2, 2020, https://slate.com/news-and-politics/2020/04/new-orleans-mardi-gras-coronavirus.html.

117 He was believed to be the oldest: John Pope, “Joseph Jenkins, Mardi Gras Indian with Guardians of the Flame, Dies at 90,” *Times-Picayune/New Orleans Advocate,* https://www.nola.com/article_f556f722-b7b9-11ea-95bc-c375419afb3c.html.

119 “The spirit hit us today”: *Mardi Gras for All Y’all:* Friday | Part 1, February 12, 2021, https://www.youtube.com/watch?v=CwdUreYn_-w&feature=emb_logo.

119 “It’s refreshing to be able”: *Mardi Gras for All Y’all,* Friday | Part 1.

120 “It’s very sacred”: *Mardi Gras for All Y’all,* Friday | Part 1.

121 “The commercial thing is more prevalent”: Kennedy, *Big Chief Harrison,* 297.

121 Harrison and his family also traveled: Kennedy, *Big Chief Harrison,* 274–75.

122 “The Black Indian wearing a dirty purple suit”: Sarah M. Broom, The Yellow House (New York: Grove, 2019), 327.

123 A cherished activity: Michael P. Smith, *Mardi Gras Indians* (Gretna, LA: Pelican, 1994).

124 Way in the morning: 79rs Gang, “Culture Vulture,” *Expect the Unexpected* (Sinking City Records, 2020).

Conclusion

128 “Nobody ain’t never gonna find the code”: “Video Interview Larry Bannock,” New Orleans Jazz and Heritage Festival, 1991, Amistad Research Center.

129 “in a variety of costumes”: Dewulf, ix.

bibliography

Books and Articles

Breunlin, Rachel, and Ronald W. Lewis, with essays by Helen Regis. *The House of Dance and Feathers: A Museum by Ronald W. Lewis.* New Orleans: UNO Press/Neighborhood Story Project, 2009.

Brown, William Wells. *My Southern Home or, The South and Its People.* Boston: A. G. Brown, 1880.

Buechler, Johann Ulrich. *Land- und Seereisen eines St. Gallischen Kantonsbürgers nach Nordamerika und Westindien . . . in den Jahren 1816, 1817 und 1818, Etc.* 1820.

Caillot, Marc-Antoine. *A Company Man.* New Orleans: Historic New Orleans Collection, 2013.

Dewulf, Jeroen. *From the Kingdom of Kongo to Congo Square: Kongo Dances and the Origins of the Mardi Gras Indians.* Lafayette: University of Louisiana at Lafayette Press, 2017.

French, Benjamin F., comp. *Historical Collections of Louisiana.* 5 vols. New York: Wiley and Putnam, 1846–53.

Fromont, Cécile. *The Art of Conversion: Christian Visual Culture in the Kingdom of Kongo.* Chapel Hill: University of North Carolina Press, 2014.

Hirsch, Jordan. "Stop Shaming New Orleans for Getting Sick from Mardi Gras." *Slate Magazine,* April 2, 2020, https://slate.com/news-and-politics/2020/04/new-orleans-mardi-gras-coronavirus.html.

d'Iberville, Pierre Le Moyne. *Iberville's Gulf Journals (1698–1702).* Translated and edited by Richebourg Gaillard McWilliams. Tuscaloosa: University of Alabama Press, 1991.

Johnson, Jerah. *Congo Square in New Orleans.* New Orleans: Louisiana Landmarks Society, 1995.

Kennedy, Al. *Big Chief Harrison and the Mardi Gras Indians.* Gretna, LA: Pelican, 2010.

———. *Chief of Chiefs: Robert Nathaniel Lee and the Mardi Gras Indians of New Orleans, 1915–2001.* Gretna, LA: Pelican, 2018.

Latrobe, Benjamin Henry Boneval. *Impressions Respecting New Orleans: Diary & Sketches 1818–1820.* Edited by Samuel Wilson Jr. New York: Columbia University Press, 1951.

Lief, Shane, and John McCusker. *Jockomo: The Native Roots of Mardi Gras Indians.* Jackson: University Press of Mississippi, 2019.

Rivlin, Gary. *Katrina: After the Flood.* New York: Simon and Schuster, 2015.

Smith, Michael P. *Mardi Gras Indians.* Gretna, LA: Pelican, 1994.

Tallant, Robert. *Mardi Gras . . . As It Was.* Gretna, LA: Pelican, 1989.

Usner, Daniel H. *American Indians in Early New Orleans: From Calumet to Raquette.* Baton Rouge: LSU Press, 2018.

———. *American Indians in the Lower Mississippi Valley.* Lincoln: University of Nebraska Press, 1998.

Waters, Eric (photographs), and Karen Celestan (narrative). *Freedom's Dance: Social Aid and Pleasure Clubs in New Orleans.* Baton Rouge: LSU Press, 2018.

White, Sophie. "Massacre, Mardi Gras, and Torture in Early New Orleans." *William and Mary Quarterly,* no. 3 (2013): 497. doi:10.5309/willmaryquar.70.3.0497.

Documentaries

All on a Mardi Gras Day. Directed by Royce Osborn. 2003. https://www.kweli.tv/programs/all-on-a-mardi-gras-day.

The Black Indians of New Orleans. Directed by Maurice Martinez. 1976. Amistad Research Center.

Guardians of the Flame: New Orleans Mardi Gras Indians. 1993. Amistad Research Center.

Mardi Gras for All Y'all: Friday | Part 1, February 12, 2021. https://www.youtube.com/watch?v=CwdUreYn_-w&feature=emb_logo.

Tootie's Last Suit. Directed by Lisa Katzman. 2009.
"Video Interview Larry Bannock." The New Orleans Jazz and Heritage Festival, 1991. Amistad Research Center.

Interviews by the Author

Agee, Stafford. July 12, 2020.
Bougere, Romeo. July 16, 2020.
Boyd, Keelian. July 15, 2020.
Boyd, Shawmika Edwards. July 15, 2020.
Butler, Ronnel. July 16, 2020.
Dave, Gilbert "Cosmo." July 16, 2020.
Dollis, Bo, Jr. 15 July 2020.
Duvernay, Charles. July 15, 2020.
Duvernay, Sadie. July 15, 2020.
Harrison Nelson, Cherice. July 21, 2020.
Wimbish, Jennie. July 15, 2020.

Court Records

John Marshall and Supreme Court of the United States, *U.S. Reports: Johnson v. McIntosh, 21 U.S. 8 Wheat. 543.* 1823. Library of Congress, www.loc.gov/item/usrep021543/.

Newspapers and Newspaper Articles

"Carnival." *Louisiana Weekly,* February 25, 1928, 6.
"The Coon Carnival." *Times-Democrat* (New Orleans), February 28, 1900.
Daily Delta (New Orleans), May 21, 1853, 6.
Daily Picayune (New Orleans), December 10, 1850, 4.
Elliott, Mary, and Jazmine Hughes. "No. 1 / Slavery, Power and the Human Cost." *New York Times: The 1619 Project,* August 18, 2019, 4.
"Maskers Visit Algiers." *Daily Picayune* (New Orleans), February 27, 1895, 2.
"Scenes from the Streets." *Times-Democrat* (New Orleans), February 22, 1871, 10.
Pope, John. "Joseph Jenkins, Mardi Gras Indian with Guardians of the Flame, Dies at 90 | Nola.Com." June 26, 2020, https://www.nola.com/article_f556f722-b7b9-11ea-95bc-c375419afb3c.html.

Albums

79rs Gang. "Culture Vulture." *Expect the Unexpected.* Sinking City Records, 2020.

Social Media

Scott, Christian. (christianscottofficial). "Happy Indigenous Peoples Day. Chief Adjuah—Chieftain and Idi of the Xodokan Nation. Black Tribes of New Orleans. Black Indians of New Orleans are Louisiana based West African tribal Chiefdoms . . ." Instagram. October 12, 2020. https://www.instagram.com/p/CGP7vMsHI0V/.